A STARS AND STRIPES PUBLICATION

CASTLES OF GERMANY

Including Salzburg

INTRODUCTION

There are more than 20,000 castles, palaces and ruins in West Germany. This book doesn't pretend to cover them all, but it does cover hundreds of the more interesting ones. And, while you may like the gilded, furnished palaces where you have to don felt overshoes before the guides will let you step on the parquet floors, don't forget that even a crumbling ruin of a castle with only a tower and fragments of walls may be still more fascinating for the children.

We have concentrated on castles in the central and southern parts of West Germany where most American servicemen are stationed. Salzburg is also included, because so many people visit that corner of Austria while they are in the Berchtesgaden Recreation Area.

April through October is the best time of year for castleering. Many castles operate on shorter schedules in winter and some close altogether. Some close down for

Important Dates, pp. 4-5   **Glossary and Index, pp. 174-176**

lunch. The best time to arrive is between 9 and 10 or just after lunch. We have tried to list opening hours wherever possible, but of course these may change.

A good source of information, particularly on castles and palaces located in towns, is the local Fremdenverkehrsverein (official tourist office), which is usually at the railroad station in larger cities and in the city hall in smaller towns. A postcard addressed to the Fremdenverkehrsverein of any sizable town will usually bring a bundle of booklets and maps in a few days.

Often, small historical booklets are on sale at the castles, but the majority of these are in German.

The bulk of the material in this book was gathered and written by Frank X. Wamsley. Other chapters were written by Peter Kuhrt and John Neumyer. The majority of the photographs were taken by Guenter Schuettler and Joe Wesley. The layout was done by Paul Fontaine and the cover and maps by Peter Jaeger.

—Barney Kirchhoff, Editor,
Darmstadt, Germany, 1967

TABLE OF CONTENTS

SIGNIFICANT DATES

58-51 B.C. Caesar conquers Gaul, expands Roman Empire beyond the Rhine, defeating Celts who adopt Roman ways.

9 A.D. Battle of Teutoburg Forest in which Germanic tribes under Hermann annihilate three Roman legions. Romans pushed back to the Rhine.

81-161 Construction of the Roman Limes (frontier wall) from near Coblenz to the Danube near Regensburg. Many castles were later built on sites of former Roman forts.

233-234 First penetrations of the Limes by Germanic tribes, forcing eventual abandonment of most of the upper Limes. Goths, Franks and Teutons quickly occupy the relinquished territory.

375-451 Tribes of nomadic Mongolian Huns invade Germany from the east, pushing Germanic tribes before them. Huns defeated 451.

406 Romans withdraw from Germany and Britain.

450-1450 Middle Ages, early part of which, the Dark Ages, lasted to about the end of the 10th century. It was during the Middle Ages that feudal lords built a great number of the fortified castles in Germany.

600 The start of Christianization of Germany by Irish monks.

800 Frankish King Charlemagne, head of the kingdom founded by Clovis in 481, crowned emperor in Rome, establishing the Holy Roman Empire. The territorial limits of the empire varied but generally included Germany, Austria, Bohemia and Moravia, parts of northern Italy, Belgium and, until 1648, Switzerland and the Netherlands. In its early history, the Holy Roman Empire also included southern Italy, France, Denmark, Poland and Hungary and nominal control over England, Sweden and Spain. Great and small principalities and duchies, kingdoms, imperial cities and ecclesiastical estates made up the empire. Since each had its own nominal head, control by the emperor was a sometimes thing.

843 Squabble between Charlemagne's grandsons results in the Treaty of Verdun, which partitioned the Frankish kingdom and resulted in the eventual formation of Germany and France as separate countries.

1050-1250 The major period of Romanesque building.

1096 The First Crusade departs for the Holy Land. Eight more crusades were to follow, the last in the late 13th century. None achieved more than temporary success in freeing the holy places, but several succeeded in taking Jerusalem, only to lose it again. It was after the Third Crusade (1189-1192) that Richard the Lionhearted was captured in Austria and later held for ransom in Germany's Trifels Castle on the Weinstrasse.

1138-1254 The Hohenstaufen dynasty attains power. Height of the Age of Chivalry, that period when Knighthood was in flower. With the election of Rudolf I in 1273, Germany had its first Hapsburg emperor and the foundation of a family dynasty which was to remain in power in Austria until 1918.

1152-1190 Reign of German King Frederick Barbarossa, the great administrator who took part in two crusades.

1198 Founding of the German Order of Teutonic Knights (Deutschordensritter). They are entrusted by Emperor Frederick II with task of colonizing Prussia and built numerous castles and fortresses.

1241 An army of Polish and German warriors defeats the Mongolians in the field at Liegnitz, thus eliminating another threat from the east.

1250 Beginning of the Gothic period, which lasted through the 15th century.

1254-1272 The League of Rhenish Cities finally succeeds in smashing the robber barons along the Rhine and wrecking most of their castles. Only Rheinfels Castle was able to withstand the onslaught.

1300-1350 Gunpowder is developed and crude cannon and small arms fired from the shoulder begin to appear. Castles gradually become unsafe under siege over following centuries as attackers armed with cannon stand back and smash the walls.

1256	Proclamation of the Golden Bull, whereby prince electors selected new emperors of the Holy Roman Empire. Of the seven princes, four held the banks of the Rhine (the Archbishops of Cologne, Trier and Mainz, and the palatine count of the Rhine); two held the eastern frontiers (the Margrave of Brandenburg and the King of Bohemia); and the elector of Saxony who controlled the heart of Germany.
1358	Rise of the German cities begins with formation of the League of Hanseatic Cities under the leadership of Luebeck. The growing economic and political power of the cities gradually weakened the feudal system and led to many conflicts between the nobles and townspeople. Many castles were besieged or sacked during such battles.
1415	Reformer Johannes Huss is burned at the stake for heresy in Constance. The Hussites War (1419-36) breaks out and spreads through Germany.
1456	Johann Gutenberg invents printing with movable type and prints the first book using this method, dealing another major blow to the feudal system.
1500	Beginning of the German Renaissance, the great revival of art, literature and learning, which began in Italy and spread through Europe between 1400 and 1600.
1517	Martin Luther nails his 95 theses on the door of Wittenberg Church (now in East Germany) beginning the Reformation in Germany.
1524-1526	The Peasants War. Bloody uprisings and pitched battles between peasants and nobility.
1600-1800	As an outgrowth of Renaissance, the Baroque style of architecture comes into fashion and is followed by the frivolous Rococo. This is also the period of great palace and residence building in Germany.
1618-1648	The Thirty Years War. Fought mainly in Germany, this conflict was between German Protestant princes and the powers of France, England, Spain and the United Provinces (present-day Holland). Sweden and Denmark sent strong forces to support the Protestant troops against their Catholic enemies. The war was also a struggle against the authority of the Holy Roman Empire represented by the Hapsburg emperors. However, there was no unity of agreement even among the Hapsburgs themselves. Fighting ranged all the way from Portugal to Austria and Czechoslovakia. End of the war saw the empire reduced to a meaningless shell and the splitting of Austria and Germany. Switzerland and the Netherlands also ceased to be parts of the empire.
1683	Turks are defeated by combined forces before Vienna, ending another threat from the east.
1689	Troops of France's King Louis XIV lay waste to the German castles along the Rhine during war pitting France against the Grand Alliance.
1701-1714	The War of Spanish Succession involves most of the West European nations in the balance of power conflict.
1740-1786	Under Frederick the Great, Prussia becomes one of Europe's most feared powers.
1792	During the French Revolution, Napoleon orders demolition of the castles along the Rhine, driving German troops across the river.
1806	Napoleon forms the Confederation of the Rhine, spelling the final end of the Holy Roman Empire.
1870-1871	Bismarck unites Germany. This introduces the era of castle rebuilding to preserve them as national monuments.

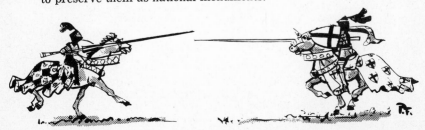

THE RHINE:
The Left Bank

THE RHINE, symbol of German patriotism, was once the boundary of the Holy Roman Empire. Many of the castles you see there today were probably constructed on the same sites upon which Roman General Nero Claudius Drusus built more than 50 forts 10 years before the birth of Christ.

When the western half of the Roman Empire collapsed in the 5th century, the Franks seized power, rebuilding and enlarging the forts abandoned by the Roman legions.

The Franks reached their peak under Charlemagne, who set up his headquarters in Aachen and reestablished the Holy Roman Empire.

When the Franks lost their grip in the 9th century, a number of independent rulers appeared on the scene. It was under these feudal lords that the great period of castle building began. During the 11th, 12th and 13th centuries, castles sprouted from almost every likely hilltop vantage point as the robber barons grew rich by extracting heavy tolls on Rhine River traffic.

Eventually, the merchants got tired of paying tribute all along the Rhine and organized an army which attacked and sacked most of the castles in the first of four great waves of destruction over a 500-year period.

Next came the onslaughts caused by the religious wars between 1582-1586, and the Thirty Years War (1618-1648).

The third and most decisive period of castle clobbering came in 1688-1689 when King Louis XIV of France, in his conquest of Alsace-Lorraine, shoved his troops all the way to the Rhine to protect his armies from the rear.

The fourth and knockout blow came in the 1790s shortly after the bloody French Revolution when French invading forces swept across the Rhine into Germany and blew up what was left of the grand old sentinels.

Let's have a detailed look at the left bank of the Rhine from Bingen downstream to Coblenz. This 35-mile stretch offers an inspiring peek into the past for those who would relive the gory Middle Ages and the glory of the Renaissance.

Sitting on a knoll above Bingen, where the Nahe River joins the Rhine, sits Burg Klopp, on the ruins of a Roman fort. The castle was built in the middle of the 10th century, then destroyed by the French in 1689 and now only the tower and some of the walls of the original castle remain.

Rheinstein Castle, near Bingen, is

Where robber barons once held sway, Rheinstein visitors like to play.

Tired of the long climb up to Rheinstein?

perched on a crag and offers a superb view of the river. Built early in the 13th century, Rheinstein was used by the robber barons until they were flushed from their roost in 1252 when the enraged League of Rhenish Cities reduced it to ruins.

Early in the 14th century, it became the property of powerful Kuni von Valkenstein, archbishop of Trier, after it was restored by the royal family of Waldeck.

Rheinstein crumbled again under the fury of the Thirty Years War and was hardly more than rubble until 1825 when Prince Frederick of Prussia acquired the property, restored it in pseudo-Gothic style and used it as a summer residence.

Less than a half-mile away is Reichenstein, which hangs over the Rhineside village of Trechtingshausen.

Emperor Rudolph von Hapsburg (1218-1291) was a great foe of the robber barons. His army knocked out Reichenstein in 1283 and had the heads lopped off the occupants as a warning to others.

Reconstructed to its present shape by 19th-century romanticists, Reichenstein is now the property of Baron Kirsch-Purcelli of Luxembourg, and houses a collection of weapons, armor and hunting trophies that trace history for three centuries.

Sooneck, the next fortified castle on the way downstream, was built above

Bedroom and nursery at Reichenstein.

Niederheimbach in 1005 by Archbishop Wiegis of Mainz. Later, it became a roost for robber barons.

A legend concerns one of those rapacious rascals, Lord Siebold, who used Castle Sooneck as his stronghold and

Partially restored in the 19th century, Schoenburg Castle houses a youth hostel.

Once-powerful Rheinfels Castle was reduced to ruins by the French in 1794.

who kept it swinging with liquid loot, kidnapped maidens and fawning cavaliers. One night, in a boastful, drunken mood, Siebold ordered two of his servants to bring from the dungeon his most recently acquired treasure—Hans Veit of Fuersteneck, also a nobleman and considered the best archer on the Rhine. But now he was without eyes. They had been gouged out by his captor.

"I understand," said Siebold, "that you can, even blind and guided only by sounds, hit a given mark with a bolt. Do so and freedom shall be your reward."

The archer was handed a crossbow cocked and loaded. The Lord of Sooneck grabbed a goblet and he hurled it to the

floor where it struck with a golden chime. "Shoot!" he ordered.

The blind archer unleashed the bolt, which struck Siebold squarely in the mouth and broke his neck. The company fled and the servants led Hans back to his home and family.

Next are two ruins, the 13th-century Heimburg, directly above Niederheimbach, and Fuerstenberg, above Rheindiebach. Both served as toll-collection stations for the robber barons; both suffered the same fates as their neighbors, and both have been partially restored. They are privately owned and not open to the public.

At Bacharach is Stahleck Castle, built in 1135 by the rich knight Goswin von Stahleck. During the Thirty Years War,

Schloss Stolzenfels has all the comforts enjoyed by nobility in the 19th century.

Stahleck and the town were captured and recaptured many times by the invading armies, and then the French leveled it almost for keeps in 1689.

Farther downstream is Oberwesel, boasting the 12th-century fortified Schoenburg, a brutish mass of ruins. Partially restored in the 19th century, it now serves as a youth hostel.

The full might of the Middle Ages is depicted in what's left of the Rheinfels castle above St. Goar. This sprawling structure was built by a famous robber baron—Count Dieter von Katzenelnbogen —in 1245. So impregnable was the Rheinfels that, when the troops of the Rhenish towns stormed it to dislodge the robers, it withstood the onslaught for more than a year.

A French army of 24,000 failed to dent the walls in 1692. In 1758, however, the garrison was surprised in its sleep and the French army grabbed it without a struggle.

The last stop on the left-bank tour of the Middle Rhine is at Schloss (palace) Stolzenfels, built in 1270 by Arnold von Isenburg, archbishop of Trier, a completely restored example of how royalty lived in the early 1800s.

Lavishly restored Stolzenfels has romantic exterior to excite castle buffs.

THE RHINE:
The Right Bank

THE GERMANS call it the Middle Rhine—that stretch of mighty river from Bingen downstream to Coblenz.

It is also referred to as the part with the most tourist appeal, because of its castles and vineyards, its myths and romantic legends and its rollicking wine festivals.

Throughout a 700-mile fling from Switzerland to the North Sea, nowhere does the Rhine River offer more breathtaking scenery on both banks than along this rugged stretch—about a 2½-hour drive on either side—without stops.

Here, the swift waters are laden with barges and triple-decked excursion boats. Wine festivals are in full swing from mid-August to mid-October. Each village, each wineshop has its own brand of "Gemuetlichkeit," making the district one of the greatest tourist attractions of Europe.

Local legend states that Charlemagne was responsible for planting the vines which now produce the superb brandy of Ruedesheim and the wine of nearby Johannisberg. The emperor, it is said, stood one winter morning on the balcony of his castle across the river at Ingelheim. When the sun arose, he noticed the snow melted more quickly on certain areas than on any of the others. He sent a servant on horseback to Orleans to collect cuttings of various vines from his French subjects. When the servant returned, the emperor was rowed across the river and with his own royal hands

Ruins of Ehrenfels Castle look down on legendary Mouse Tower in river.

he planted the French grape seedlings in the German soil. Three years later the first grapes were harvested.

When the wine was ready it was the color of gold and was served the emperor in a golden goblet. It became his favorite drink and "it made him young again in his old age." Visitors to the district who would like to sip a wine fit for a king should try that fiery Johannisberger, known as "the king of all Rhine wines."

One of the best ways to view this gorgeous gorge is to approach it from Wiesbaden on Route 42. The gateway to the Middle Rhine is Ruedesheim on the right bank. It is here that the high river banks become nearly vertical, screening out cold winds and permitting the sun to create a climate that is somewhat milder than average for Germany.

This gorge runs for about 25 miles downstream and boasts more castles than any other river valley in the world.

Of the three castle ruins near Ruedesheim, the lower castle—Broemserburg —is the one most worth a visit. The Romanesque castle served for centuries as a fortified residence for the archbishops of Mainz and later for the strong-arm knights of the robber Baron Broemser, a 9th century gangster who clipped barge skippers and merchants for a 10 per cent levy on their goods.

It offers an interesting museum of

The fortified Pfalz, midstream at Kaub, was a toll station of the robber barons.

Terraced vineyards above St. Goarshausen make a perfect setting for Castle Katz.

wines, drinking vessels and wine-making gear.

In the river below Ruedesheim, you will see the Mouse Tower, a toll gate once controlled by the wicked Bishop of Hatto. He tricked a band of protesting peasants into entering a barn which he then set afire. Millions of mice are said to have emerged from the burning structure.

They chased the bishop, who fled by boat to the tower. The hordes of mice pursued him to the tower, nibbled through the massive doors and devoured the evil man.

High on rocks above Ruedesheim lies the Niederwald Forest and a tremendous monument, the symbol of German unity —"The Lady With the Sword"—erected by Bismarck in 1870. It is also known as "The Watch on the Rhine."

A short distance downstream from Ruedesheim is the charming village of Assmannshausen, famed for its red wines, outdoor restaurants, wine-sipping establishments and top-flight restaurants.

That noble mass of ruins you see just before Assmannshausen is Ehrenfels Castle, a visit to which is not worth the difficult side-trip. It was built in the first half of the 13th century and destroyed by the French in 1689.

Proceeding downstream, one reaches Kaub, which boasts the most extensive vineyards of the Middle Rhine. It is also the location of another midstream fortified toll station—the Pfalz—built by Louis the Bavarian in the 14th century.

Above Kaub on the hillside towers a remarkably well preserved fortification —the Gutenfels Castle, which dates back to about 1235. At present, it is used by an industrial firm for the training of

Marksburg Castle stands high on a crag over the village of Braubach and the Rhine.

apprentices and is not open to the public.

After leaving Kaub, you near the site of one of Father Rhine's most delightful legends—the Lorelei. She was the river siren who is said to have lured sailors to their deaths with her crooning.

Although there's nothing to see but a sheer cliff of gray volcanic rock, her legend attracts millions who are lured by her echo—a phenomenon induced by tourist voices when the wind is right.

There is a fine view from the top of the sleeping siren, which you can easily reach by car.

Next we drive down to St. Goarshausen where Castle Katz stands guard on the hillside. It was built by Count Johann von Katzenelnbogen (Cat's Elbow) at the end of the 14th century. It resisted all invaders until it was destroyed in 1804. Restored in the early 1900s, it is now a boys' boarding school and is closed to the public.

Castle Katz has a downstream neighbor named—you guessed it—Castle Mouse, above the town of Wellmich. Its construction was begun in 1353 by the electors of Trier. The counts of Katzenelnbogen scornfully referred to it as the "mouse" that would eventually be devoured by the "Katz."

Architecturally, the Mouse is one of the finest of the fortifications along the Rhine. It was carefully restored between 1900-1906 and is now owned by a Berlin industrialist. Nope—no visitors.

The next formidable ruins we see are Sterrenberg and Liebenstein—the "enemy brothers" castles, built almost side-by-side, but separated by a wall and a moat as a result of a feud between two noblemen who had a falling out over the favors of the same princess.

Both of these castles were destroyed by the French in 1688. Towers and walls remain and there is a restaurant and a car park.

Next, a cloud-bumping crag high above Braubach, is the Marksburg Castle, the only fully preserved medieval fortress on the Rhine. It changed hands successively from the powerful House of Eppstein in the 12th century to the counts of Katzenelnbogen who had it until 1479, then to the Landgraves of Hesse until it was captured by the Prussians in 1866. In 1899, Kaiser Wilhelm presented Marksburg to the Association for the Preservation of German Castles, which owns it to this day.

Marksburg is a delight to lovers of medieval lore and romance. It offers a truly authentic picture of the fortified and domestic culture of those old days.

Collections of armor, uniforms and weapons lure tourists to the mighty Marksburg.

THE RHINE:
Coblenz to Cologne

THE LOWER RHINE, from Coblenz to Cologne, has a bit of everything for the castle-and-palace buff—from medieval fortifications and torture rooms to Rococo palaces.

Since Caesar's time, the tide of European history has ebbed and flowed up, down and across the Rhine. Through the Middle Ages, the Reformation, the French Revolution, the Franco-Prussian War and into the 20th century, thousands have died in countless battles for control of that vital waterway.

Probably the most famous spot on this stretch of the Rhine is the Ehrenbreitstein Fortress, which looms over Coblenz from the top of a 385-foot cliff across the river.

Fireworks and floodlights rekindle the romantic spirit at famed Ehrenbreitstein.

The bastion was billed as impregnable. And it usually was. But sometimes attackers used their heads instead of their halberds and simply starved out the besieged defenders.

Starvation defeated the fortress twice —during the Thirty Years War when German troops let hunger decimate the French stronghold, and during the French Revolution, when the tables were turned. That time, French troops kept German defenders under siege for five years (ending in 1799) before the famished remnants finally hoisted the white flag. The French destroyed the fortress in 1801.

Though Romans built fortifications on the hill, Ehrenbreitstein's recorded history started in 1019, when Ehrembrecht (which slowly became corrupted to Ehrenbreitstein) of the Salish-Konradish family owned it.

Like most Rhine castles, it changed hands several times and was destroyed, rebuilt and destroyed again. The last major reconstruction was completed in 1832 after 17 years of work by the Prussians.

Today, the main bastions and old prison are still standing.

The fortress now houses a youth hostel, a restaurant and a museum with exhibits covering Ehrenbreitstein's history back to Caesar's times. Unfortunately, one of the castle's most famous pieces is now at the Invalides in Paris. It's a mammoth cannon built in the 16th century that shot a shell weighing 142 pounds. It required 94 pounds of gunpowder to fire the cannonball.

From the courtyard, the panorama of the Rhine is breathtaking. So is the view of the Eifel and Hunsrueck Mountains—on a clear day.

The fortress can be reached by car, if you like narrow roads; by chairlift, if you like open-air view; or by foot, if you like mountain climbing.

The museum is closed every Friday and from Oct. 15 to March 1.

For another view of the Rhine—and of its rich history—cross the river to Coblenz and drive 17 miles north on Route 9 to Burg Rheineck, another castle on whose foundations the footsteps of 2,000 years of history are visible.

It's located on what was once the

You can see some interesting weapons, like this flail, at Rheineck Castle.

Rheineck Weapons Room window displays coats-of-arms from robber baron days.

frontier between Caesar's Roman Empire and the barbaric tribes of Germany. The Limes—the Roman defensive line which stretched from the Rhine 400 miles to the upper Danube to protect the provinces to the south—started across the river from Rheineck.

The Franks probably used the hill down through the centuries, but its place in the history books starts in the 10th century with the first Count Otto of Rheineck. Unfortunately (for him), Otto picked the wrong time to side with the Bavarians in their feud with the Swabians. Swabian King Konrad III took over the castle and had it torn down in 1152.

The archbishop of Cologne got control of the property and started rebuilding the castle in 1164. Only the floor of the chapel remains from this effort.

But the castle grew in importance and became one of the four key strongholds of the archbishopric of Cologne (there wasn't any concern about separation of church and state in those days). The archbishop made the knights of Ulmen lords of Rheineck and 17 counts of this line ran the castle for the archbishops— a long reign considering the times.

The soldiers of Louis XIV of France plundered and burned the castle in 1689.

It was rebuilt (1837-40) by a Bonn professor who liked the location. The present castle is the fifth structure built on the site.

There was a Jewish community at the foot of the mountain from the Middle Ages and the cemetery, though almost hidden by underbrush now, was used until 1878.

The Rheineck tower draws visitors like a magnet. It dates from Carolingian times and, according to the guide, is 1,200 years old. Like the keeps of most castles, it housed a dungeon and was used as a last redoubt for defenders.

It now contains a collection of armor from the 12th, 13th and 16th centuries and a torture chamber with several grisly reminders that methods of persuasion may have been crude in the old days, but undoubtedly were effective.

The view takes in several miles of river and the ruins of Hammerstein Castle across the river as well as Arenfels Castle, which is privately owned.

Also visible across the river is Burg Ockenfels. It is one of the many German castles which have been transformed into hotels. It's 1½ miles north of Linz.

At Bad Godesberg, 6 miles south of Bonn, is Godesburg Castle. Or what's left of it.

Only a few walls and the tower remain, but a modern restaurant has been built on the site. It was designed by Cologne architect Gottfried Boehm, and completed in 1961. Its aesthetic lines successfully link the past and present and enhance rather than detract from the ancient walls.

The castle was first built about 1210, although a shrine was located on the hill in Roman days. The archbishops of Cologne used the castle as a residence.

Like many strategically placed castles, Godesburg was tough to knock over. Or was until 1583 when Duke Ernst of Bavaria was named archbishop of Cologne. A Gebhard Truchsess opposed his appointment and put up a fight at Godesberg.

Ernst's brother Ferdinand besieged the castle unsuccessfully for about a month and then, in desperation, turned to his "secret" weapon.

He dragooned some Eifel miners into digging a tunnel through the mountain. The duke exploded 1,500 pounds of gunpowder under the castle and the wall came tumbling down.

It was rebuilt but destroyed again by the French in 1794—for the last time.

For a change of castle-hopping pace,

Flamboyant Bruehl Palace is now used by West German government for state affairs.

the palace in Bruehl is worth a stop, particularly if you're a student of the Baroque and Rococo periods of European architecture. Today, it's used by the West German government for important state receptions.

A succession of archbishops built residences and castles on the site during the Middle Ages. After French troops destroyed it in 1689, Bruehl entered its richest period, thanks to Archbishop Clemens August, who had a taste for the good life and apparently could afford to patronize a stable of artists.

In 1725, he commissioned the palace, called Augustusburg, to be built on the site as a monument of Baroque splendor.

But styles change and so did the arch-bishops' artistic tastes. From 1728 to 1770, no less than five architects and interior decorators tried their hand at pleasing the archbishop and his successor. Their efforts ranged the gamut of architectural styles of the day.

Despite Clemens August's lack of consistency, the palace is an excellent, well-maintained example of the flamboyant period, from its intricate parquet floors to its elaborately frescoed ceilings. Among tourist favorites are the floral gardens of Dominique Girard and the lavish, multi-colored marble staircase of Balthasar Neumann.

It's open daily from 7:30 am. to 6 p.m. but is closed during December and January.

Grand staircase at Bruehl is the extravagant creation of famed Balthasar Neumann.

THE MOSEL:
History Flows Like Wine

PERHAPS THE MOST delightful aspect of the Mosel River is that along its verdant flanks today's traveler may see and touch history as it was made, revel in remnants of the past, and follow the growth of civilization from Roman times to the present.

In Germany, the Mosel wreathes its charms for 120 miles through Trier to Coblenz before it joins the Rhine and submerges its identity.

Among the first to develop the Mosel area was Caesar Augustus, who, in 15 B.C., brought grapevine shoots, walnuts, fruits and flowers to grace the river's slopes and meadows. He also brought bronze and iron tools and weapons to build and protect fortifications.

The Mosel has carried wines and warriors down to the Rhine and helped haul barges laden with great blocks of stone

A fire signal basket hangs high over the 12th century Burg Thurandt walls.

quarried by slaves of Emperor Constantine in 39 A.D. to build his summer palace at Neumagen. The Mosel ferried invading armies back and forth from one bank to the other, from those early Roman conquests, to the bloody engagements of the Middle Ages, on up to the times when German imperial troops tangled with the French armies of Louis XIV.

Today the Mosel, still the same highway it was when the Romans brought civilization to Germany, is one of the world's greatest wine-producing districts.

Wine would seem to be the Mosel's greatest tourist attraction, then castles, museums and health hotels. Each village has its Probierstuben (wine-tasting inns), its own classic labels and vintages.

The nearly perpendicular, vineyard-covered slopes that confine much of the Mosel were formed by prehistoric volcanic eruptions that lathered the banks with layers of molten slate. Subterranean fires heated the pleasure palaces of the Romans who boated, bathed and binged along the river. Those hot springs still flow through the plumbing of today's Mosel spas. The healing waters at Bad Bertrich remain at a constant 89 degrees, while Bad Wildstein boasts 95.

Historical delights adorn the Mosel, from the mighty Roman Porta Nigra in Trier to the ruins of fortified castles, and castles that have been restored. Worth special visits are Burg Eltz, Burg Thurandt and Burg Cochem.

Venerable chapels include those of Longuich Gothic Church and its 15th century "Madonna of the Grapes"; the ancient vintners' chapel of St. Nicolas in Loersch; the carved altars of the Leiwen parish church, and St. Peter's Chapel in Neumagen.

At Zell, the palace of the electors, built in 1542, is perfectly preserved and is now a hotel and restaurant.

Each village along the Mosel has its private legend, work of art, link with an ancient culture. Bernkastel-Kues has its Renaissance marketplace, pillory and fountain. At Traben-Trarbach is Louis XIV's excavated fortress and the ruins of the once-great fort of 12th century Gravenburg.

To get the most from a Mosel trip the traveler should be equipped with one of

Storybook Eltz Castle was strategically unimportant and escaped the ravages of war.

those accordion-type panoramic maps available in English at all souvenir shops along the river. The map indicates important historical features, agricultural data, distances and sights worth seeing.

Of the dozens of the Mosel's fortified castles that were built to defend their noble owners, only three today are intact. The other knighted shrines, whose innards have collapsed and have never been restored, are hardly worth more than a moment's pause. But you must pass beneath their unpeopled parapets, which still exude a solemn dignity, even in decay.

From Coblenz, it's best to take the right (south) bank of the Mosel, since the first castle you will "storm" will be Burg Thurandt at Alken, which lies 15 miles upstream. A yank on the iron bell-ringer at the gate will summon an attendant to let you in.

When the gate creaks closed, you find yourself in a creepy passage in the hush of the year 1192 when the place belonged to Henry, son of Duke Henry the Lion of Saxony and Bavaria (1129-1195). The son died in 1227 and the ownership passed to another son, Holy Roman Emperor Otto IV, who reigned from 1209 until his death in 1218.

There has been much restoration over the years and the Middle Ages atmosphere has been retained in the parts that are habitable.

Interiors accessible to visitors are completely furnished with museum pieces from the styles of living over eight centuries.

There is a collection of armor and

The Reichsburg at Cochem has a secret passageway which guides show to tourists.

hunting trophies, hand-written Bibles, tapestries and a chapel, original hand-hewn oak floors and ceilings.

After Burg Thurandt, the castle tour continues upstream to Brodenbach where, if one is addicted to ruins for the sake of ruins, one may visit what romanticists proclaim "the most beautiful castle ruin on the Mosel."

We take you now to the storybook Burg Eltz, back in the hills on the other side of the Mosel, probably the only castle you'll ever walk DOWN to. You'll gasp with pleasure at your first glimpse of it from the cliff—grasping an iron railing to keep your vertigo from hurling you downwards—as it sits on a knoll down there between your perch and another mountain.

Burg Eltz is so far from roads and the Mosel and is of such strategic insignificance that it was never ravaged. Louis XIV hurled his troops toward it in 1689, but issued a last-minute reprieve

through one of his generals, Duke Louis Francois Bouffiers (1644-1711), then a marshal and peer of France.

Another remarkable feature of Burg Eltz is that it has been owned and lived in by the same family for the past 800 years. Built in 1160, it housed four families of the Eltz clan. The present descendants use it as a summer residence.

Burg Eltz is completely furnished as a museum and as a monument to 800 years of one family's life from the dark ages through the 18th century. One runs the delightful historical gamut of the Eltz family tree through oil paintings of wigged, noble forebears, fireplaces, stoves, utensils, furniture, tapestries, bedrooms, hall of the knights, and the weapons and tools of the times.

The children's bedroom offers a point of special interest.

"The floors are a mixture of oxblood, cow hair and clay," intoned the guide. "And the, how-do-you-call-it, plaster?

Cochem commands the Mosel's steep slopes, believed formed by volcanic upheavals.

The wall plaster is made of a mixture of ox blood and cheese."

Subsequent investigation revealed that Middle Ages builders made a very strong form of cement and plaster. They used animal blood as a binder combined with skimmed-milk cheese and adhesive clay from the marshes (or from dried fresh curd) added to quick lime and a little camphor. Animal hair reinforced the mixture.

To visit the third and last of our medieval Mosel castles, we must now proceed to the Mosel and upstream to Cochem, topped with Burg Cochem, also known as the Reichsburg. This stunning structure dates back to 1027 when it was an imperial residence.

The interior is lavishly furnished with works of art gathered from conquests that included the Middle East.

There is a secret passage. The guide trips an invisible plunger with his foot. A panel in the library wall creaks open and reveals a moldy, ancient stairway that winds down eerily into the bowels of the burg.

To reach the castle one must park in the village and find the right street. There are no guide signs. The road is paved all the way up but it's restricted to visitors on foot.

21

BERWARTSTEIN:
The Knights Came Up the Chimney

CASTLE CONNOISSEURS who want their castles to look like a picture from a fairy tale will find Burg Berwartstein in the southern Rhineland-Pfalz tailored to their taste.

Its position on a pinnacle gives it a 360-degree command of valley approaches. In its early days, the castle could have been defended by one man. The only entrance to the rock fortress was through a chimney-like aperture on the east side. Wooden steps let down into the opening could be drawn up and the defender could pour boiling oil, pitch, lead or whatever was at hand down onto assailants.

This method of defense must have had loopholes however, or else the defenders were starved out, because eventually the knights of Berwartstein who owned the castle from 1201 to 1343 lost it.

These knights were robber barons who terrorized the southern Pfalz as far away as Strasbourg during the 13th Century, according to history pieced together from records in the Speyer archives.

Finally, the cities of Strasbourg and Hagenau pooled their resources and stormed Burg Berwartstein. The knights put up a good fight but finally surrendered and sold their castle to the brothers Ort and Ulrich von Weingarten.

During the next couple of hundred years, the castle changed ownership several times and the Fleckenstein family occupied it for three generations until fire gutted the interior in 1591.

Capt. Theodor von Bagienski, known as Hoffmann, restored the landmark to livability between 1893 and 1922. The walls had remained intact—but the interior was a shambles.

Then a Dane took over. Aksel Faber acquired the castle in 1922, but since he spent much of his time in Mexico and Denmark, he persuaded Alfons Wadle of the nearby village of Erlenbach to care for the castle.

Erlenbach itself is one of the first known villages in this area of forested hills, fertile valleys and picturesque "chimney rock" outcroppings. It dates back to 740. The castle is believed to have been started before the village was founded, although no records exist prior to 1152.

Wadle bought the castle in 1955 and did most of the restoration from World

Clouds hover eerily around Burg Berwartstein, said to be haunted by a "white lady."

War II damage with his own hands. While he owns it, it is under supervision of Landesamt fuer Denkmalspflege (office for preservation of national monuments) and the exterior must remain unchanged.

Theo Wadle, son of Alfons Wadle, conducts tours. "I grew up right here," he said. It is "home" for him, his wife and two children and his parents. They maintain a private residence there.

The Knights Hall, an arched salon with magnificent views from its windows, and frescoed walls showing knights in armor, is still used as a dining room. During July and August hot meals are available during the week but only on Sundays in less-busy seasons.

Although the "chimney" through which the owners entered in olden days has been blocked off within the castle, you can step into the bottom of the vertical shaft which is ventilated by several natural openings on the way to the top.

From Heidelberg and Mannheim, the best route to Burg Berwartstein is by way of Speyer, Landau, Bergzabern, Erlenbach. From Kaiserslautern-Ramstein-Sembach go via Pirmasens, Hinter-Weidenthal, Dahn, Erlenbach. Signs point the way to the castle from Erlenbach.

The castle is open daily from mid-March to mid-December.

If you have time for a side trip after seeing Bewartstein, drive eastward to Dahn. Along the way you'll see fantastic rock formations that have given this area the title "The Poor Man's Dolomites."

Mountain climbers clamber among the wierd crags, and tourists like to be photographed waving from precarious platforms. The most exciting of these outcroppings is the Drachenfels (Dragon Rock) which is entered through a tunnel and ascended by a stairwell hewn inside the boulder, the base of which is only half the size of the flat top.

Hovering over Dahn is what appears to be the remains of a mighty two-towered fortress. These are the ruins of two 11th century castles, Alt Dahn and Grafen Dahn, separated by a deep ravine and scowling at each other.

A short distance down the road is Neu Dahn. In 1603, the Dahn line became extinct and the whole works went to the bishop of Speyer. During the Thirty Years War, the barons of Waldenburg took over. Retreating French armies laid all three Dahn castles to waste as they played their final trump in the 17th century.

In early days, this narrow "chimney" was the only entrance to the castle.

A steel-nosed battering ram brings home power of ancient siege weapons.

23

THE SAUERLAND:
A Tempestuous Past

THE BUCOLIC QUIET of the Sauerland is a pleasant contrast to the booming, industrial Ruhr, a few miles west, and is one of the few areas of Western Europe where a foreigner still is something of a novelty.

Its rolling, forested hills, neat fields and pastures is real get-away-from-it-all country, but the rustic atmosphere belies the Sauerland's sometimes-tempestuous past. The castles which top the hills overlooking its strategic rivers have seen many a battle and many a war come and go.

Castle hunting takes a bit more snooping in the Sauerland, but a little curiosity and a touch of doggedness will pay off.

Massive Schloss Burg now is a palace.

It's an area abounding in medieval fortresses. A few worth taking in are:

Schloss Burg, the castle converted into a palace; Altena Castle, well-stocked with armor; Schnellenberg Castle, now a fine hotel; Waldeck Castle, boasting of a witches tower and dungeon; and the big, Baroque masterpiece, Arolsen Palace.

Big Schloss Burg is one of the easiest to reach — a few miles west of the Cologne-Hannover autobahn near Solingen in the town of Burg. The castle, which dates from the 12th century, was painstakingly rebuilt between 1890 and 1915 by a private group of castle buffs, the Association for Maintaining Castle Burg on the Wupper River, which gathered and catalogued an excellent collection of artifacts and memorabilia and recreated a medieval atmosphere in the castle's rooms. Worth a trip themselves are the Claus Meyer murals in the Knight's Hall and Ladies' Salon, depicting significant events in the castle's history.

Though Burg is called a Schloss (palace), it's really a Burg (castle). To further confuse the semantics, it was first built by a fellow named Berg — Count Adolf I von Berg — in 1118.

And, of course, it's located on a Berg (hill) in the town of Burg.

Its reason for being at first was strictly military. Then **Count Engelbert II,** an archbishop of Cologne, converted Burg in the early 13th century into a large palace. It was a favorite residence of the Von Bergs through the 14th century. During the Thirty Years War it was destroyed, then rebuilt slowly.

The Berg family apparently wasn't content to remain around Burg, however. One of them, Adolf III, took over the territory around Altena in the late 12th century and with it, the castle.

To reach Altena, take Route 229 from Remscheid, north of Burg, about 17 miles east to Luedenscheid, then turn left to Altena.

Tucked in a narrow, winding river valley, the town of Altena fits the character of the castle looking down on its narrow, twisting streets. It's a town which hasn't quite caught up with the automobile age. The road to the castle is not easy to find and the one "Zur Burg" sign is equally difficult to spot.

Between 1906 and 1915, the castle was rebuilt in its original form by a private organization.

The castle's walled, cobbled entrance and courtyard have a medieval ambience. Its museum, in the form of re-created rooms and a chapel, is well-stocked with weapons, furniture and armor from various periods. It's closed Mondays.

Though not as dramatic as the Rhine's past, the history of the Sauerland nonetheless has been well-washed by the tide of events.

There's Neuenhof Castle south of Luedenscheid, but it is in private hands and not open to the public.

Wittgenstein Castle, near Laasphe, is now a private school, also with no visitors allowed.

Berleburg Palace, at Berleburg, is semiprivate, and not worth an extra trip.

But Schnellenberg Castle is — particularly for a relaxing weekend.

Take Route 54 from Siegen to Olpe, then another 9 miles to Attendorn. Signs will direct you from there.

Schnellenberg has belonged to the Fuerstenberg family since 1594.

It was once the most powerful fortress in the Sauerland. From the 13th to the 16th century, it swapped hands several times between the church and Schnellenberg family.

Vase in Schloss Burg's Collection.

Statue of Count Adolf I, dressed for battle, who started on Burg in 1118.

In 1594, Caspar von Fuerstenberg bought the castle and a new chapter of its history began. He was highly intelligent and ambitious. He had studied law and, by 1570, already was a special envoy and adviser of the elector of Cologne. He began a 14-year reconstruction of the castle in 1595.

Though Caspar used the castle as the center of his fief, his descendants later resided at Adolphsburg and Herdringen. In 1889, a fire destroyed part of the castle and it remained in ruins until 1931, when Count Wenemar von Fuerstenberg began a restoration. A small museum, with artifacts collected by the family, is open on request.

Waldeck and Arolsen Castles are over on the eastern side of the Sauerland. Waldeck is southwest of Kassel about 20 miles. It may also be reached by taking Highway 252 north from Marburg and turning east when the road passes the big Lake Eder. This same road continues on to Arolsen which is west and somewhat north of Kassel.

Knights sometimes were a bit errant about documenting their real estate —

there's nothing about Waldeck in the records until 1120 when the counts of Waldeck apparently owned the castle. The counts of Schwalenberg took over about 1178 and lived there almost 500 years.

If its location helped the occupants keep visitors out in the old days, it is now helping to bring visitors into the hotel and restaurant within the old castle walls. The castle looks down, down, down to the man-made Edersee and out to the rolling, forested hills beyond.

The Edersee wasn't always so peaceful looking. In May 1943, its dam was one of three blasted by the British RAF and its then-secret weapon—spinning bombs.

When the Eder Dam split open, 200 million gallons of water roared down the steeply sided, narrow valley with a terrifying rush.

Waldeck Castle is not much easier to reach now than it was during the Seven Years War (1756-1763) when the French conquered it. But the trip is worth it, particularly if you yearn for quiet and some good fishing (the pike and perch strike heavily on the lake).

Waldeck's collection of artifacts is small, but its museum includes a "Star Chamber," a tower dungeon and a cramped cell where a Swedish officer was imprisoned for seven years during the Thirty Years War. He had made the mistake of revealing the secret of the castle's water supply.

Off the ancient "courtroom" is the Hex Tower containing a lightless dungeon where prisoners were fed through a

The charming cobbled courtyard at Altena Castle leads one to the museum (below), with its crossbows and armor.

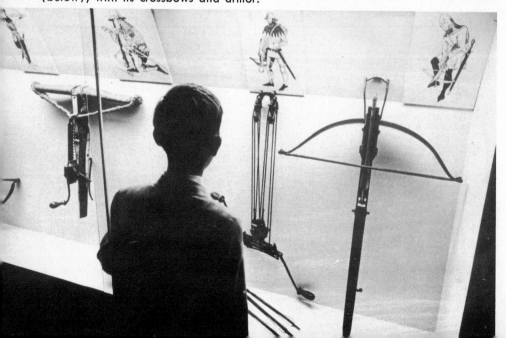

hole in the ceiling. It dates from the 14th century.

Unlike many of the Rhine castles, Waldeck is off the strategic track and has had a relatively peaceful history.

If you go for Baroque, you might like to check Arolsen as long as you're in the neighborhood. It's a half-hour drive.

There was a nunnery on the site from about 1130 but in 1526, during the Reformation, Count Philipp III evicted the nuns and converted the buildings into a fortified castle with a moat and high walls.

The present palace got its start in 1710 under Prince Friedrich Anton Ulrich. He had the old Renaissance castle torn down and commissioned a new palace along the lines of the Palace of Versailles.

It was finished in 1728 but his successors also had some ideas about interior decoration (it apparently was the men, not the women, who were fickle about such things in the old days) and added to the furnishings.

The palace and its museum have a collection of art and furnishings from many eras, and are considered among the finest examples of Baroque architecture in Germany.

Arolsen is in private hands and is open only by appointment.

The beautifully restored Schnellenberg Castle is a popular honeymoon spot.

Waldeck Castle looks down on peaceful Lake Eder, scene of a big RAF bombing.

THE LAHN:
Limericks and Landmarks

Hessian costumes are on display in Biedenkopf Castle. Marburg Castle (below) overlooks the charming city.

THE LAHN River's main claim to fame is a medley of ribald limericks extolling the virtues and vices of the proprietress of a riverbank inn.

And sure enough, there's a string of busy establishments up and down the river, each cheerfully claiming to be the original "Wirtshaus an der Lahn."

But don't let this confuse you—there's plenty to see and do along the Lahn, especially for castle connoisseurs.

A right-bank tributary of the Rhine, the Lahn winds its way for 152 miles past such Hessian towns as Marburg, Giessen, Wetzlar and Limburg.

For an easy one-day tour, you could work your way downstream by starting with Biedenkopf Castle, 21 miles northwest of Marburg on Route 62. It's small and unpretentious but its museum contains an excellent collection of period folk costumes in tableaus of family life.

Marburg Castle is inextricably intertwined with German religious history, first as the home of St. Elisabeth and then as a focal point of the Reformation.

It was of strategic value as far back as the 11th century when a Franconian watchtower was located there. Here Martin Luther, Philipp Melanchthon and the Swiss reformer Huldreich Zwingli met in 1529 in a vain attempt to conciliate their Protestant ideologies.

Thanks to the vicissitudes of war, the huge structure has undergone m a n y changes — from Romanesque through Gothic to Renaissance. Most noteworthy are the small, but impressive Gothic knights' hall, with its vaulted ceiling, and a chapel in the south wing which is considered a jewel of High Gothic church architecture.

Marburg itself is a charming old town —full of medieval delights — with the other principal landmarks being the university and St. Elisabeth's Church, the first Gothic cathedral in Germany.

From Marburg, Route 3 runs alongside the Lahn to Giessen, passing Friedelhausen Castle, privately owned and a youngster as castles go. It was built in 1850 in the English Tudor style. A little later on, the road takes you past two castle ruins towering over the hills, Frauenberg and Staufenburg.

At Giessen, pick up Route 49 and drive past Wetzlar (renowned for its 12th-century cathedral and old town section).

The next stop—and you shouldn't miss it!—is Braunfels, a picturesque village of 3,900 nestled around Braunfels Castle. You'll be able to see it miles away, jutting far above the rolling Lahn countryside.

The castle contains a well-stocked museum and has been in the possession of the counts of Solms-Braunfels for centuries. It is currently occupied by Prince Georg and his clan.

An historic note: Prince Georg is a descendant of the man who in 1842 founded New Braunfels, Tex., with a group of German settlers.

The museum collection includes suits of armor and weapons; an art gallery with Italian, Dutch and German works, medieval sculpture, and religious paraphernalia.

Continuing on Route 49, the next-to-last stop should be Weilburg, a town which can say that "Napoleon slept here" in the Baroque castle. Once the residence of the dukes of Nassau, the magnificent structure has been completely restored to its palatial splendor, which includes a French garden.

You can end your trip by getting on the autobahn at Limburg, renowned for its bulky cathedral which is worth a quick visit. You'll get the best view of

Braunfels Castle . . . a link with Texas.

the imposing 13th-century structure—and a final look at the lazy waters of the Lahn—in crossing over the autobahn bridge.

Napoleon once slept in Weilburg Castle, home of the dukes of Nassau.

SAALBURG:
Bastion on the Roman Iron Curtain

THE IRON CURTAIN is nothing new to Germany. In fact, fortified lines running through the country date back to the 1st century.

Rome's m i g h t y empire stretched through Europe to the British Isles and it was no snap to maintain the sprawling frontiers. Not many years after Christ's Crucifixion, Julius Caesar expanded his domain along the Rhine River.

Unable to push the empire to the Elbe River as planned, the Romans fell back and built a fortified line reaching all the way from Coblenz to Regensburg.

Called the Limes Germanicus, this "Little Iron Curtain" evolved from simple earthenworks to wooden palisades and even, in places, masonry walls with all the defensive refinements those times could offer.

Backing up the Roman "curtain" were forts where legionnaires manning the L i m e s lived and stored their supplies, relatively safe even from the not-infrequent breachings of the fortified frontier.

One of these forts was at Saalburg, lying atop a long, low ridge in the Taunus Mountains not far from the resort town of Bad Homburg. It was built a couple of hundred yards behind the Limes and was the center of a thriving little community.

Like the castles of later days, it provided refuge in times of crisis for the civilians who lived nearby. Outside its

Roman shoe made of stitched leather was found in the ruins at Saalburg.

walls were baths, a village, temple and cemetery, the remains of which may still be seen.

Another similarity between the Saalburg and a castle is that it has a moat. Not of the water-filled variety, it is dry and consists of two concentric ditches around the walls.

Much of the old fort was carried away in the Middle Ages by peasants seeking building materials but enough was left to spur a campaign to acquire funds to restore this relic of Roman times. Government and private sources (including American) chipped in and work got under way in 1898. It was completed in 1907.

Architects did their homework carefully, studying documents and drawings

Drawing shows how the Castell looked in 120 A.D. with Limes running nearby.

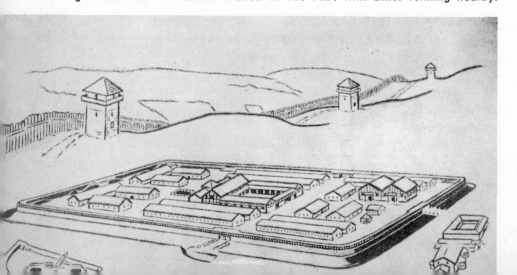

of ancient times, and the result was a near-perfect example of a Limes Germanicus fortress. Today, castles may be a dime a dozen but the Saalburg is a rarity for the European sightseer.

A road built by the Romans still leads to the main gate (porta praetoria). A footbridge crosses the defensive ditches and, by the gate, is a bronze statue of Emperor Antoninus Pius holding a staff topped by the Roman eagle.

One of the first things to be seen inside is the reconstructed barracks buildings. About 500 soldiers were garrisoned in the Saalburg and, from the time of Emperor Hadrian (117-138 A.D.), they were the 2nd Cohort of Raetians.

A reproduction of the granary is used as a museum. It contains one of the finest collections of Roman artifacts to be found in Germany.

There are large pottery vessels, spear tips, piles of daggers, lances, horseshoes, wheels, tweezers, pliers, needles, combs, mirrors, rings, leather sandals, forged iron tools and implements. Many of the items on display were fished out of wells in and around the Saalburg.

In the center of the fort is the headquarters building and drill hall. The

Emperor Hadrian looks over courtyard adjoining the regimental cult "chapel."

biggest wing of this building would be large enough for assembling men in formations. It now contains some fearsome relics of Roman weapons, including a crossbow-like device which could fire a heavy spear more than 300 yards.

Adjoining the drill hall is an open courtyard surrounded by a wooden colonnade. At the far end is the regimental chapel (sacellum) in which the cohort's standards, the military chest and official cult images were kept.

On each side of the courtyard were armories and heated rooms, probably used by the equivalent of company commanders and first sergeants of those days. They contain curios assembled from Roman ruins at Feldberg, Stockstadt and other places.

The woods and fields around the Saalburg are dotted with ruins and earthworks, the purpose of some still unknown. The mystery of it all—and a large picnic ground — makes this area particularly inviting during the pleasant months of the year.

Museum is filled with Roman artifacts, many found in the fortress' wells.

THE TAUNUS:
A Silver Leg and a Saddle Stool

KAISER WILHELM'S saddle-shaped writing stool, the "silver leg" of the Prince of Homburg, a Charlemagne stronghold and a colossal ruin which once had central heating.

These are some of the delights of a castle tour just north of Frankfurt and Wiesbaden. Practically within muzzle-loader range of each other are about a half-dozen castles.

Let's start off with Homburg-under-the-Hill, in the spa town of Bad Homburg. The castle was a summer residence of the German emperors from 1866 to 1918.

It hasn't been definitely established when the various parts of the palace were built, except that it occupies the site of a 12th-century castle of which only the so-called White Tower remains. There lived Friedrich II, a tough, able monarch who reigned from 1680 until 1708 and won high honors as a cavalry general in the services of Sweden and

Friedrich II may look soft but he was a fine general of the cavalry.

Brandenburg. He was immortalized by poet Friedrich Schiller in his play "The Prince of Homburg."

A cannonball smashed his leg when he was 26, but a skillful craftsman fashioned an artificial limb with a silver ankle joint. It was so well made that Friedrich's superior horsemanship never suffered. The leg is now on display in the castle.

Also on view are the emperor's comparatively plain bed, his writing stool in the shape of a small saddle, his water-flushed toilet ingeniously concealed in a wardrobe, and a pint-sized bowl and pitcher which served as a lavatory.

To continue, follow the road to Oberursel and Kronberg.

The former palace of the eldest daughter of Queen Victoria of England it survived World War II unscathed, and was requisitioned by the U.S. Army until 1951.

Kronberg made headlines in 1946 when the castle's WAC club officer and an Army colonel were charged with the theft of Hesse's royal family jewels and heirlooms, worth more than $1.5 million. Both were sentenced to prison terms and dismissed from the service. Most of the jewels were never recovered.

The 80-room palace was turned into a posh hotel in 1954 and the lush grounds around serve as a golf course.

From Kronberg, take the road that links up with Route 8 to Koenigstein, another Taunus spa. The town is dominated by the Koenigstein fortress, an imposing hulk worth a short visit.

Chances are that the castle — with its yard-thick walls and huge fortifications — would still be standing if it weren't for the French who in 1796 assigned a 30-man demolition squad to fill the castle well with gun powder and mine the walls. The charge went off prematurely, blowing everything and everybody to high heaven.

For another touch, head for Eppstein and its namesake castle, once the home of the Counts of Eppstein.

After the Thirty Year's War, the castle fell into disrepair and served as a quarry for everybody who happened to need a few granite blocks. Alarmed benefactors put a stop to the destruction by buying the ruins in the 19th century, and in 1929 it became municipal property.

There's a small historical museum in the former chapel and again a tower.

Friedberg Castle, about 15 miles straight north of Frankfurt, in its heyday was a heavily fortified hamlet complete with residences of the castle's lords, moats, drawbridges, gates and watchtowers.

At the northern end of the city of Friedberg, the castle occupies the site of an ancient Roman garrison. It was a Frankish stronghold under Charlemagne and later reverted to the powerful Stauferns who incorporated it into their castle chain under Emperor Frederick Barbarossa.

Many of the original castle buildings have remained standing, and so have the massive walls, two gates and the stubby Bergfried (keep) the oddly silhouetted watch tower which has become the landmark of Friedberg.

Muenzenberg is a colossal fortress ruin considered one of the most important in Germany in regards to its Romanesque architecture.

To get to the farming village of Muenzenberg and its mighty landmark, take Route 455 from Friedberg to Berstadt and follow the Muenzenberg turnoff from there. You'll be able to see the fortress from miles away.

Muenzenberg was built in the second half of the 12th century by the Von Hagen clan. Historians have established

Adolf's Tower is landmark
of the Friedberg Castle and town.

that, unlike most fortresses which were cold and clammy the year around, Muenzenberg was one of the best heated castles anywhere. They discovered three separate heating systems: open fireplaces, Roman-style floor ducts, and a two-story round tiled stove.

Koenigstein Fortress is an imposing hulk of a ruin destroyed by the French in 1796.

GELNHAUSEN:
A Study in Contrasts

THEY'D RATHER FIGHT than switch in the good old days of yore and maybe that's why there are so many ruins of castles in Germany.

Ruins are more romantic, say those imaginative souls with enough creative instinct to people decayed battlements with archers and cobbled courtyards with knights in armor. Maybe so.

But the conjuring act won't work for people who demand their medieval relics intact, not in ruins.

Whichever you prefer, the area around Gelnhausen, Germany, can fill the bill. In the city you'll find the remains of a 12th century fortress built by none other than Emperor Frederick I, or Barbarossa because of his red beard.

About 11 miles northwest of Geln-

Barbarossa's old castle in Gelnhausen, built on soft soil, decayed to ruins.

hausen are the semi-restored ruins of the 700-year-old Ronneburg Castle dominating the meadowed Hessian countryside. Only another five or six miles northeast of Alt Wiedermus (where Ronneburg stands) is Buedingen with its nearly perfectly preserved castle and museum.

Barbarossa's red sandstone fortress on an island in the Kinzig River at Gelnhausen long ago fell into decay but there's enough left to excite the imagination.

The emperor ordered the castle built not long after his election in 1152. The exact date is unknown but the castle and its enclosed palace were finished by 1170.

The main gate to the Kaiserpfalz, as it is called, leads through a columned entryway beneath what was the imperial chapel. The chapel was used for many years after the castle had ceased to be of defensive importance.

If you stand in the gate house, the castle's ruined keep (the original entrance is about 20 feet up) is on your right. The six-foot-thick walls swing away in front of you in a graceful semicircle disappearing on the left behind the ruins of the palace.

Originally, the palace had three stories, with the upper two fronted by a series of rounded arches and a flight of wooden steps leading from the main (second) floor into the courtyard.

Ronneburg Castle may be a bit more to your liking if Barbarossa's ruined fortress seemed to be more notable for what is lacking than what remains.

Stop in the 13th century well-house and take a look into a well which goes down 273 feet. Lights installed on the rock face of the well at the 125- and 260-foot levels give those who fear falling a bit of a jolt.

Much of the castle was destroyed by a fire in 1621 which left only a shell of half of the principal buildings. The upper gatehouse and some other parts were rebuilt in 1654 but most of the ruined structures lay exposed to the weather for 200 years.

Ronneburg is owned by Prince Otto Friedrich von Ysenburg and Buedingen. Since 1467, this castle and the one in Buedingen have been in his family.

The Ronneburg Castle was built in 1231 but was burned 10 years later.

Traces of this first bastion are still evident.

For the next 200 years, the castle grew until its inner buildings, gates, outer walls and other fortifications presented a formidable obstacle to invading armies.

For the better part of the 14th century, the castle was a nest of robber barons who preyed on caravans headed west to Frankfurt.

Dozens of rooms in the castle are open to the public. They contain such items as a fine collection of 18th-century muzzle-loaders, t w o - h a n d e d swords, battle-axes and halberds, crossbows, saddles, primitive agricultural implements, spurs and horseshoes. They are spread over four floors connected by a spiral staircase.

Originally a moated castle, the Buedingen castle was built in the closing years of the 12th century by Hartmann von Buedingen, a follower of Barbarossa.

In 1247, the castle was turned over to the Ysenburgs, who have retained possession of it.

The Hercules Hall at Buedingen offers a Baroque sleigh, and faded murals.

The bitterest period in the castle's history was the Thirty Years' War in which the counts of Ysenburg took the Protestant side and were severely beaten and driven into exile. When they returned, they declared their holdings open to all religious beliefs.

The prince's family and guests reside in an entire wing of the castle and use most of the rest. Tours of the castle take you through 10 rooms, several of which are in daily use. The dining room, for instance, shows how the family still enjoys its meals in the grand fashion.

Lovers of antique firearms will find an armory full of beautifully inlaid and etched muskets and rifles. Laid out in showcases so they can't be touched, these weapons almost without exception are collector's items.

A small room in the museum wing is set up as a 16th-century alchemist's laboratory. You pass through it on your way to the chapel, a gem of early Gothic architecture, about 500 years old.

Big treadmill enabled Ronneburg garrison to hoist water out of the 273-foot-deep well.

DARMSTADT:
Porcelain and a Moat in the Middle

One entire room of the Darmstadt Palace is devoted to medals—pre-1914 vintage.

A MASSIVE castle ringed by a deep moat in the very heart of the city and the smallish Prince Georg Palais

Moat and the city surround the palace.

nearby are just about the only reminders that Darmstadt was once the royal capital of Hesse.

Both structures suffered severe damage in World War II.

It took years of painstaking work and hefty investments to restore both buildings to their pre-war appearance, but for a city robbed of most of its historical edifices the efforts were necessary.

Little could be done about the rich furnishings and interiors of the downtown castle which were lost in bombing raids. The largest sections of the rebuilt edifice have been reserved for state archives, the university library and a police station.

But, in 1965, the Darmstaedters finally opened their Schloss Museum, a 10-room complex filled with antique treasures either saved from the fire or collected from other Hessian castles which are not to be restored.

The castle stands on the site of a 14th-century fortress erected by the counts of Katzenelnbogen. In the last half of the 16th century, Landgrave Georg I built a Renaissance structure there, and in 1671 a bell tower was added.

In 1722, Landgrave Ernst Ludwig commissioned a French architect, Le Rouge de la Fosse, to round out the construction with the massive wings facing the market square.

Despite this downtown splendor, the

Prince Georg Palais has a priceless collection of about 6,000 pieces of porcelain.

town itself had not much to offer. Tradesmen and other burghers who had to travel through derisively referred to it as "Armstadt" (Poorsville).

Then Landgrave Ludewig X, who called himself Grand Duke Ludewig I after 1806, took over the rule and immediately started to improve the overall picture of Darmstadt, as well as the lot of its citizens.

He stimulated municipal growth, added churches, schools, and an opera house, and commissioned several smaller chateaux and palaces.

The museum offers a glimpse of Darmstadt's regal past. There's a display of art and furniture from the Renaissance, Baroque and Louis XVI periods. One room is devoted to medals and decorations from European and Asian nations, all of pre-1914 vintage.

In the hall behind the entrance, you'll be surrounded by 15 carriages and coaches dating from the 18th century. The largest coach—a gold-finished, velvet-padded model with leather springs and wooden wheels as standard equipment—seated four in discomfort. Allowing for the bad roads of that time, even dukes had to experience mild forms of torture riding in such a vehicle.

A recent addition to the displays are the colorful uniforms of Hessian regiments, and other military equipment.

Topping the tour is a visit to a room which contains a 1526 painting of the Madonna and Child by Hans Holbein the Younger. The picture has never been retouched or refinished, according to Ernst Hoffman, museum director.

The other Darmstadt castle, the Prince Georg Palais, is worth visiting for other reasons. After extensive renovation it was reopened in 1951 with a priceless collection of porcelain.

Among the 6,000 pieces displayed here are items from all over Europe and the Far East.

The grand duke of Hesse began collecting the porcelain from castles and palaces in 1907 and opened the museum in 1908.

In 1943, the duke's son transferred the treasures to a wine cellar near Oppenheim to protect them from bombing raids. Just before the end of World War II, the collections were taken to a flour mill in the Odenwald where they survived with every piece intact.

Among the most interesting pieces are flea legs, little porcelain boots about three inches long which were filled with honey to trap bugs under ladies' petticoats.

KRANICHSTEIN:
Dedicated to the Hunt

JAGDSCHLOSS Kranichstein, a combination pleasure palace and hunting lodge, witnessed the playboy antics of many an eccentric Hessian ruler, but the gent who perhaps was the most Baroque of them all was Grand Duke Ludwig VIII, known as the "greatest nimrod of his time."

Ludwig (1691-1768) was not only an ardent hunter; he did things in the grand style—like driving through the forests in a conch-shaped coach drawn by six red deer stags.

Kranichstein is a treasure house devoted for nearly 400 years to the worship of Diana, goddess of the hunt. One can trace the history of the chase, from crude 15th century bows and spears to the gamut of muzzleloaders—the matchlock, the wheelock and the flintlock—as well as the Baroque period when the amount of inlaid ivory, gold and silver on the gunstocks determined one's status in the sporting set.

Kranichstein was built in 1572-78 by the first of the great Hessian lords of the chase—Grand Duke George I. The lodge was the scene of much gaiety at the beginning and end of every hunt. In fact, the idea was so popular that in 1700 Grand Duke Ernst Ludwig added a 110-yard-long wing and an arsenal. Gradually the lodge assumed grander proportions as successive rulers, whose veins effervesced with royal blood lines from the time of Charlemagne, left their signatures to posterity.

Ludwig VIII in 1740 stuccoed the walls and hung priceless paintings from the art capitals of Europe. Soon the place became well known as a Lustschloss (pleasure palace). It offered as much in comfort as any famous spa of the era. So sumptuous was the place that even Queen Victoria recuperated there.

Kranichstein was dedicated to pleasure and joys of hunting.

Hunting became such a way of life at Kranichstein that artists were commissioned to put on canvas the exact conditions under which boars and stags were brought to bay.

Kranichstein, just outside Darmstadt, carries on the hunting tradition with its Falkenhof (falconry), adjacent to the Jagdschloss. Surrounded by a high fence, it is home for falcons and hawks as well as some American golden eagles and a pair of wise old owls.

The noble bearing of the falcon—a bird prized as a symbol by medieval nobility —is enough to excite any observer and

---

Other falconries in Germany are:
Burgfalknerei Hohenbreitstein at Heilbronn; Falknerei Starkenburg above Heppenheim on the Bergstrasse between Darmstadt and Heidelberg; Falkenhof Falkenlaut at Bad Ems on the Lahn River; and Adlerwarte in Berlebeck at Detmold, northwest of Kassel.

---

this is just the place to see a demonstration of this ancient art.

German emperors indulged in falconry after they learned about it from Arabs during the Crusades and the sport flourishes to this day. Hunting small game with birds of prey is believed to have originated in China about 2000 B.C.

The falconry welcomes visitors to performances of its birds every Saturday

Famous 32-point Battenberger stag was brought down at Kranichstein.

from 2:30 to 4 p.m. during the warm months of the year.

Among Jagdschloss exhibits, aside from collections of 600 period weapons, spears, bugles, etc., are the carriages used to transport the stags and boars to the hunting area, where the beasts were released and chased.

In 1917 the last grand Duke of Hesse Ernst Ludwig collected every hunting memento from castles throughout the duchy and stored them in Kranichstein. With World War II the proud place changed from sybaritic to utilitarian and it became a home for the aged. At war's end it became an art school for art and holiday music classes. In 1953 it was acquired by the Hessian Society for the Preservation of Castles and restored to the appearance it displayed in 1750, during the reign of Ludwig VIII.

That's the way you'll see it today, inside and out, except that now it also boasts a fine restaurant and modern plumbing. The palace is open to tourists all year except in January.

A falconry is adjacent to the Schloss.

Demonstration of a falcon's skill.

THE BERGSTRASSE:
Towers, Monsters and a Dragon or Two

THE BERGSTRASSE is an ancient Roman trade route that winds along the base of the Odenwald between Heidelberg and Darmstadt. Its charm lies in medieval remnants of historic dwellings around which the modern villages have grown; the hills that tower above it are dotted with gaunt, crumbling towers whose tenants were once monarchs of all they surveyed.

Of the nine or more castles that one views while driving along the Bergstrasse, there isn't a single fortress that is much more than a shell. None survived the bloody conquests of 17th century religious and political w a r s except one. Frankenstein, perched above the Eberstadt section of Darmstadt, was spared but simply went to its knees from neglect.

The Frankenstein family of knights built their castle overlooking Eberbach and Nieder-Beerbach early in the 13th century. The family split into two lines, but lived there together quarreling over property rights, hunting rights, taxes and toll fees. They eventually sold out to the Hessian royal family in 1662. The Hessians converted it into a home for retired mercenaries.

Later, Louis the XIV of France laid the countryside to waste and the castle became a refuge for homeless villagers.

When the wars were over the villagers went back to their ravaged homes, taking every movable implement and stone with them. There are still some mighty walls and towers and the place is worth a look.

The name Frankenstein alone is

Frankenstein Castle
survived wars then fell into ruins.

A tree grows high atop wall
in the ruins of Auerbach Castle.

The palace at Weinheim now contains public offices but gardens are a real delight.

enough to incite a chill and to entice the traveler.

Almost everyone knows that Frankenstein was the title of a novel written in 1818 by Mary Wollstonecraft Shelley, wife of the poet, and whose main character created a monster that destroyed him. Frankenstein castle has no connection except the name, but it does have enough spooky corners to let your imagination run riot.

A legend more closely connected with the castle concerns the son of Philip von Frankenstein, a knight named Sir George. According to the story, a brook flowing through the nearby town of Nieder-Beerbach was the home of a hideous dragon. The dragon terrorized the townspeople and refused to desist unless the natives offered in sacrifice the fairest maiden in the valley. Annemarie, a forester's beautiful daughter, known as the "Rose of the Valley," was chosen.

But just before she was to be delivered, Sir George returned from a crusade, fell in love with the maiden at first sight, learned of her plight and rode out to engage the fire-breathing reptile. After a furious fight he dealt the critter a deadly blow. In its death throes it managed to insert the tip of its poisonous tail through the hinge of George's knee armor, mortally wounding the heroic knight. George was reportedly buried in the little church in Nieder-Beerbach. Annemarie spent the rest of her days in a nunnery.

The next ruin you'll spot south of Eberstadt is more hidden than the rest but it is visible through the trees on the Alsbach hillside. There is a magnificent view from the 12th century ramparts.

The Auerbach Schloss, looming over Bensheim, has an immense dignity that is worth the climb.

Its drawbridge and moat have felt the tread of mailed feet since 1257, and its ponderous walls and towers defied the clawing of the elements and wars until the French and Swedes gnawed away at it during the Thirty Years War (1618-48) and finally sacked it.

Farther down the road at Weinheim you'll see the towers of Wachenburg and Windeck. Windeck is mossy ruin that was a proud fort in 1102 and remained so until — you guessed it — the French leveled it in 1674.

On a neighboring hilltop is the Wachenburg. But it is not a castle. Its foundation formerly belonged to a fortified edifice but the present structure is a modern youth hostel.

Weinheim itself should be visited, if only to walk through the Schloss Park and to look at the Lebanon cedar that was planted there in 1730.

The palace, built in 1537 and enlarged through the years, is intact and houses the city hall and police department. A fine restaurant is on the grounds and there's a mini-golf course. The grounds are shaded by magnificent trees and famous for its exotic plants.

On the grounds of the Weinheim Schloss is the "Blue Hat," a 15th century prison tower still intact.

THE ODENWALD:
Sanctuaries and Ivory Carvers

CENTRAL GERMANY has a plot of lovely real estate stretching north from the Neckar in the direction of Darmstadt and Aschaffenburg called the Odenwald. In this beautifully forested area, traces of man from some of the earliest prehistoric periods have been found.

Along the northern reaches of this region there grew up a number of castles, partly to protect timbering rights and partly to protect the trade routes from the south.

Three of these castles, Lichtenberg, Otzberg and Breuberg, played a part in the Thirty Years' War and provided sanctuary for people fleeing the armies.

Farther south in the Odenwald, Lindenfels and Erbach also offer castles.

Lichtenberg Castle and the town bearing the same name are perched on the

Lichtenberg castle is built near the site of an ancient Celtic fortress.

saddle of a ridge amid a cluster of hills and small mountains, some of which are higher and more impressive. It is believed to have been erected about the turn of the 13th century.

To the southwest, a much higher range of hills overshadows Lichtenberg. Here, you can make an interesting side trip to view the remains of a Celtic fort built at least 100 years before Christ's birth. One of three such earthworks in the Odenwald, the partially preserved Heuneburg, like its castle neighbor, was a place of refuge in times of war.

Some of the relics from this ancient ruin as well as a collection of Roman relics found in the Odenwald may be viewed in the small museum in Lichtenberg Castle. It's closed, however, from Nov. 1 until Easter.

Facing the inner defenses is the open end of the horseshoe-shaped palace, itself a part of the defenses, built by Count George I of Darmstadt, 1570-1581.

About the only spot where you can get a good overall look at the castle is from the squat tower (49 feet high and 58 feet across) a few hundred yards away on the other side of the town. It was built as a gun platform to modernize defenses after the advent of gunpowder.

Most of the remaining rooms are rented to local families; and they have plenty of natural light because the palace has a window for each day of the year.

Following the route taken by the famed Minnesingers — those warbling troubadours of yore who sang their way to the top of the medieval ballad parade — and the ill-fated Nibelungen, to say nothing of Celts and Roman legionnaires, we come to Otzberg Castle. Originally, it was called Ottosberg after Emperor Otto but subsequently acquired the shorter name it now bears.

From Lichtenberg, take the road through Gross Biberau, Reinheim, Lengfeld and Zipfen. About a mile beyond Zipfen, a narrow road turns west toward the village of Hering, which has grown up on the base of the hill on which the castle perches.

A round keep — a tower designed to provide "last-resort" defense — stands centered between the inner walls.

There was a Roman colony on this site until nearly the end of the 3rd cen-

Beautiful stucco work in the Knights' Hall is a highlight of the castle at Neustadt.

tury when the Franks drove the legionnaires back to the Rhine. King Pepin, the first Carolingian king of the Franks, gave the place to the monks of the abbey at Fulda in the eighth century but it was not until the beginning of the 15th that the present fortress was begun.

Ponderous gate is at Breuberg Castle.

In 1511, it was rebuilt and strengthened; a strong gate house with drawbridge and moat were added and the outer ring of walls added. A 260-foot well provided water in times of need but even all this did not save Otzberg in 1647 when French troops conquered and plundered town and castle.

Other than the walls and the keep, there's little left of what once stood in the Otzberg. What didn't fall over the centuries was pulled down. A goodly portion was broken up and carried off in 1826 and may be seen today in several of the public buildings in nearby Gross Umstadt.

The smaller building by the gate contains a restaurant, open all year, and quarters for the regional forester.

The next stop on your castle tour is Breuberg. From Hering, head east to Hoechst, take Highway 45 and continue east to Neustadt where signs in the middle of town point up the hill to the castle and parking area.

As you enter the double-arched gate in the outer walls, you'll see a small cannon pointed in your general direction. It's the only piece of artillery you'll see here, so feast your eyes.

It is written that in the 16th century, 20 cannon and 60 smaller fieldpieces were sufficient for the castle's defenses.

The keep rising out of Breuberg's deeply shadowed inner courtyard approaches 120 feet in height and is surely one of the most massive in Germany.

No one knows when the first fortification was erected here but, like its neighbor Otzberg, Breuberg was on land giv-

43

Erbach offers fine display of armor . . .   . . . and even some for your tiny tots.

Beautifully hammered 17th century saddle was brought to Erbach from Milan, Italy.

en by King Pepin, father of Charlemagne, to the abbots of Fulda in 766.

The nucleus of the present castle was in existence in 1160 and before the 15th century it had become a permanent residence of nobility.

Well worth seeing, aside from the Roman artifacts collection in a primitive sort of museum, is the stuccoed ceiling in the Knights' Hall. A beautiful relief work, done between 1610 and 1624, the ceiling depicts the seasons and scenes from classical mythology and Aesop's fables.

Vis-a-vis from the museum building is a restaurant and, in the warm months of the year, tables are put in the courtyard for diners.

Much here is in ruins but there's plenty left to stimulate the imagination of the romantic-minded.

The chapel goes back to the earliest days of Breuberg but has been remodeled a number of times. It is still used and retains a sparse unmistakable medieval atmosphere.

Return to Highway 45 and go south until you come to Erbach with its palace built by Count Franz I in 1736. The founder of Erbach's ivory carving industry, Franz filled his palace with an armor collection, Roman and Greek antiquities, a huge collection of hunting trophies and rare and valuable pieces from many periods.

A man of vision, Franz I introduced many reforms to modernize his backward "kingdom." He died in 1823 but some of the changes he wrought live on today.

Group tours are available but cameras are prohibited inside. Heavy felt slippers are provided to protect the floors—and they're mandatory.

While in the area, stop in Erbach's sister city of Michelstadt, whose timbered town hall is one of the most photographed sites in Germany.

Lindenfels, the "pearl of the Odenwald," is not far to the west on Highway 47. The ruined castle there looks down on the quaint little town from its hill.

Damaged in the Thirty Years War, it got the coup de grace when French troops hit the walls with everything they had in the 17th century. Scavengers of building materials did the rest and only a shell is left today.

Quaint town square in Michelstadt is a target for many tourist cameras.

Wars and scavengers haven't left much to see of the Lindenfels Castle.

HEIDELBERG:
It Still Goes Up in Flames

THERE'S a curse on Heidelberg Castle. At least that's what the fishwives used to say in the Old Town marketplace.

The hex was called early in the 15th century, venting its wrath on the castle and its tenants through the bloody Reformation period, the Thirty Years War, the Palatinate War with France and a series of destructions by lightning and fires that kept the curse alive until 1764.

Today, old Heidelberg Castle sags with tired elbows like an exhausted monarch on its redstone knees, but it still dominates the old town and the Neckar Valley with a stubborn, royal dignity.

Partly inhabited, it still boasts lovely gardens, intact Baroque halls, charming 15th century fireplaces and collections of pewter, porcelain and furniture.

Apart from the romantic stones, one of the big attractions today is the world-famous Heidelberg Tun—a huge wine cask with a capacity of more than 50,000 gallons. It's in the three-story Tun Wing next to the Ladies Wing where the great festival hall is located.

The parapets and buttresses are silent now; the former tenants are harmless life-size figures hewn from stone.

And the whole works goes up in flames again several t i m e s each summer when the keepers reenact the castle's destruction by the French in 1693.

The curses began around 1415 when Bohemian Protestant reformers John Huger, John Huss and Jerome of Prague were burnt at the stake in the Constance marketplace for heresy at the command of Palatine Elector Louis III.

It is said that a witch in the crowd screamed for heavenly vengeance on the ruling prince and his successors and for the castle to be destroyed with hellfire.

A short time later, Louis' wife, an English princess, died of a mysterious illness. Their son and heir to the throne died before he was 21.

When the Bavarian-Palatinate War ended in 1507, Elector Ludwig V built some of the castle's finest wings, many of which stand intact today.

Heidelberg Castle and city "go up in flames" commemorating destruction of 1693.

Model graphically illustrates the glory that was Heidelberg before its destruction.

Elector Otto Heinrich took over the castle in 1556, contributed another of its sections, but died childless three years after his succession. "It is God's will our line should die out," he mourned. "Our founder stained himself with the blood witnesses of the truth."

The curse really began swinging when Elector Prince Frederick V made the scene in 1610. He brought with him as his bride, Princess Elizabeth Stuart, only daughter of King James I of Great Britain and Ireland and granddaughter of Mary, Queen of Scots.

Frederick nearly died of smallpox and had another close brush with death when someone poisoned his meal at a gathering in Heilbronn.

In November 1618, the curse came in person in the form of a great comet. In its wake came the Bohemian conflict and the Thirty Years War from 1618-48, the battle of White Mountain near Prague, where Frederick and his army were clobbered by Count Johannes Tilly. Frederick lost his crown, was stripped of his dignity as prince of the Palatinate and was declared an outlaw by the emperor.

Elizabeth fled to Holland. In 1622 Tilly

Frederick Wing of the castle was constructed in the 17th century.

Medieval chemists laboratory in Heidelberg Castle is one of the finest you'll find.

stormed Heidelberg Castle, and looted it of all of Frederick V's royal possessions after having pounded its stalwart walls with artillery for weeks.

In 1623, Frederick died of plague, leaving Elizabeth widowed at 35 after having borne 13 children.

Rival claims for the royal reins to the Palatinate sparked the War of the Palatinate Succession in 1689. In this tilt, the French destroyed Heidelberg and the castle and blew up the powder tower.

The curse seems to have taken a breather for the next few years. New rulers came and went after having left

Big touristic attraction is the Heidelberger Tun—a wine cask with 50,000-gallon capacity.

Oil painting depicts scene of terror and confusion as French put town to the torch.

their marks in rebuilding the battered old schloss.

In 1764, just about the time the mess was straightened out, the castle was again struck by lightning and the destruction was enormous. It was partly restored again at the end of the 19th century.

Despite great destruction of the 17th century, the castle still has much to offer sightseers.

THE WEINSTRASSE:
Crowned With Noble Ruins

GERMANY'S Weinstrasse has 50 miles of grapevines, villages, restaurants, wine shops—and romance.

From a crest of forested hilltops, noble ruins peer down upon the traveler as though to say: "Come up and see me."

Roofless, crumbling, and naked except for choking vines, those ruined castles suffered the same fate during the same years by the same hands. Of more than 200 such structures scattered throughout the Rhineland Pfalz, the Weinstrasse (Wine Road) offers an interesting assortment.

Tell the kids that those massive walls and towers once had roofs, royal tenants and housed fabulous collections of jewels and priceless loot from conquest. Tell them that these castles suffered, aside from constant local squabbles, four great waves of destruction: (1) The wrath of the League of Rhenish Cities, which finally overthrew the robber barons along the Rhine; (2) The Thirty Years War which involved the armies of France, Sweden and Spain; (3) The onslaught of French King Louis XIV in 1688-89; and (4) The French Revolution in 1792.

Gruenstadt is considered the northern end of the Weinstrasse, because that's where the Rhine Valley slopes up from the plains and it's this grape-terraced rift that furnished the excuse for hilltop castles and which separates the vintners from the dairying flatlanders.

Running south, you'll come to such interesting sights as the Karlbacher Castle, once an important trade route guardian; Alt Leiningen Castle, built by a crusader in 1100; Limburg Abbey, which was converted from a fortress; Hardenburg Castle with its 23-foot-thick walls; the Wachenburg, a real sandstone skeleton of an old warrior; the impressive ruins of Hambacher Schloss, started in the 10th century; the Kropsburg near Maikammer — its stones were carried away and sold; Madenburg Castle, a great place to camp for the night; and Landeck Castle, the oldest of all, which was built by Landfred in the early 5th century.

But the star of the show on the Weinstrasse is Burg Trifels, once the Fort Knox of the Middle Ages. It was built early in the 11th century to store treasures wrested from other German rulers.

Its most famous resident was held in the castle's plush prison for 13 months.

Richard the Lionhearted was kept prisoner in massive Burg Trifels for 13 months.

That was King Richard the Lionhearted of England, who cooled his heels there (1193-1194) while waiting for his family to pay the ransom demanded by Henry VI.

Richard was returning from a crusade when he was captured by his arch-enemy, Leopold of Austria. Henry paid Leopold 60,000 silver marks (about $190,000) to get Richard and then, craftily, demanded 150,000 marks ransom, which the English paid.

Much of the legend is disputed but the story of how the troubadour Blondel found Richard by playing his lute beneath the walls of castles will forever live in romantic history.

Trifel's first tenant was Conrad II (990-1039), ruler of the Holy Roman Empire. When he completed the box-shaped structure he promptly stuffed it with the loads of loot he snatched when he defeated the duke of Lorrain.

Aside from being the vault that contained the emperor's crown, jewels, scepter, complete treasury and regalia of the monarchs, Trifels was a sanctuary where uneasy royal heads could recline safely when trouble lurked.

When Conrad III became emperor in 1138 he founded the Hohenstaufen dynasty, and under them, Trifels underwent its greatest development.

The castle, in 1523-24, was ravaged by rebels in the Peasants War; in 1602 it was struck by lightning, which destroyed its great tower and a huge section of the battlements. During the see-saw Thirty Years War of 1618-48 it was repeatedly captured and recaptured.

By the time Louis XIV of France came through Germany in 1689 there was nothing left of Trifels but shelter from a storm, and he blew it up along with all the rest of the castles in the Pfalz during the Battle of the Great Alliance against the Germans.

Today Trifels has been restored. Upwards of 2.000 visitors trudge the narrow trail daily—twice that number on Sundays—to view the bare walls and floors of the three-tiered structure and to admire the monumental halls and staircases of pink sandstone.

Of particular interest to the visitor "(Where was Richard kept?") is the top story, which contains the Lion's den —a huge dining hall, a bedroom and study where the English monarch languished in luxury. On the same floor is a small museum displaying centuries-old coins and a tabletop model of Trifels as it was supposed to have looked when completed in the 11th century.

Old print shows a disguised Richard being taken captive by the Austrians.

Town hall has replica of imperial crown, once part of Trifels treasure.

51

KARLSRUHE:
A Dream Palace

DREAMS COME TRUE—sometimes. Anyway, one did in Karlsruhe and, legend tells us, that's why there's a gorgeous palace there today.

Karlsruhe Palace is one of four palaces (plus a sprinkling of castle ruins) the burg buff will want to view in this corner of southern Germany.

According to the Karlsruhe legend, a wealthy German prince got lost while out stag hunting. He fell asleep while resting under an oak tree and dreamed of a fantastically lavish palace.

Upon awakening, the prince found his way to his ancestral home. From there, he sent heralds far and wide with a message to his subjects: "Come to me with your families and belongings. In return for your skills, I will give you 10 years of freedom from statutory labor, military service and taxes and you will receive free lumber and free land on which to build your homes."

His subjects responded with such alacrity that, in no time at all, the prince was ensconced in his fan-shaped palace surrounded by vast beds of exotic flowers and trees, pheasant preserves and herds of deer.

That's how romanticists describe the origin of Karlsruhe Palace, which was conceived by Prince Karl Wilhelm of Baden-Durlach on June 15, 1715.

Today it is obvious that the palace of Karlsruhe (it means Karl's Rest) is neither legend nor dream. The fabulous structure was completed in 1775, a fan-shaped Shangri-la from which radiated noble houses of art and science as well as royal dwellings for the court.

Bombed in 1942, it has been restored to its original form, except for a modern interior which more befits its current function as home of the Baden State Museum.

Among its treasures are the famed Turkish weapons and war trophies collection of Duke Ludwig Wilhelm; coin collections and minting machines; Etruscan, Greek and Roman artifacts; and important archeological finds from the Upper Rhine that disclose the way of life from ancient to modern times.

A few miles south of Karlsruhe lies the city of Rastatt, with its Versailles-

Old print of Karlsruhe shows how streets radiate outward from the central palace.

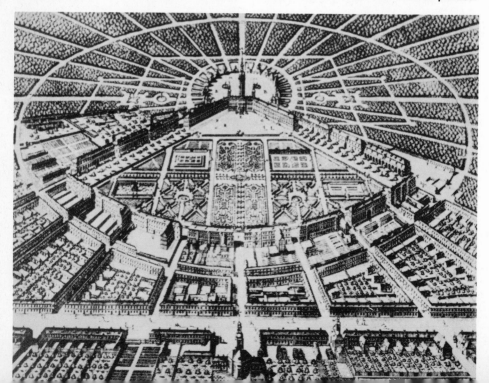

Once-glittering Baden-Baden Neues Schloss now houses a fine museum.

like pink sandstone palace. Schloss Rastatt was built in 1700 as the residence of the dukes of Baden-Baden. It was the scene of the Congress of Rastatt in 1789, which resulted in Germany's loss of the left bank of the Rhine to France.

Once famous for its wild, jubilantly rampant stucco work, the palace's somber facade faces a king-sized formal

Clock in Karlsruhe Palace Museum.

garden. One wing houses a small collection of Renaissance doodads but the major portion of the palace is not open to the public.

Just east of Rastatt, near Kuppenheim, is the Schloss Favorite, built by eccentric Duchess Sibylla Augusta of Baden-Baden in 1725 after the death of her husband Duke Ludwig Wilhelm.

The palace is a fantastic integration of imported marble, furniture, Chinese silk wall coverings, porcelain, chandeliers, inlaid floors, precious stones and, for inclement weather, a reception hall designed to accommodate her highness' coach-and-four.

A short distance south lies Baden-Baden, a bath town founded by the Romans and the ancestral home of the grand dukes of Baden-Baden who reigned from the Middle Ages well up into the 19th century.

Perched over the city is the Old Castle, now only a rugged skeleton of its former might. Built early in the 13th century on the sight of a Roman outpost, it served as a mighty fortress until 1479, when Margrave Christoph I decided to build a new castle and gave the old home to his dowager mother. French forces destroyed both in 1689.

The New Castle became a palace in the late 16th century. Margrave Phillip II commissioned the most highly skilled craftsmen of the times to design and install imperial dining rooms, balustrades, reception salons and a coach house.

In 1805, the palace was partially restored, but the big housecleaning came in 1843-47, when Grand Duke Leopold, a romanticist, restored the palace in the brilliant style of the Phillip II epoch.

It is now a historical museum housing vast collections of the Baden rulers and branches of the family.

THE NECKAR:
A Necklace of Towers and Fortresses

THE MOST romantic stretch of the Burgenstrasse—Germany's Castle Road that begins at Heidelberg and winds its way to Nuernberg—is probably along the Neckar River valley.

Just like the Rhine, the riverbed is flanked on both sides by haunted fortresses, castle ruins and towers which peer down with the dignity of a glorious and bloody past.

Going upstream, the first concentration of castles comes at Neckarsteinach which boasts no less than four and is therefore also known as "Vierburgeneck"—Four Castles Corner. The two best preserved—the Mittelburg and the Vorderburg—are both privately occupied and do not welcome tourists. The Hinterburg is a small, uninteresting ruin, and only the Schwalbennest (Swallow's Nest) above town is worth a climb for a good view all around.

Neckarsteinach was one of the points along the river where robber barons stretched chains across the stream and forcibly extracted tolls from barge skippers.

Across the Neckar, you'll see a conical hill topped off by a tiny, heavily fortified hamlet. This is Dillsberg, stronghold in the 11th century of the counts of the Elzengnau. The fortress, now in ruins, resisted the armies of the imperial general Tilly in the Thirty Years War and those of the French as late as 1799.

To get up on the hill, you'll have to cross the river at Neckargemuend a little farther downstream, but the view of the valley on both sides is worth it.

A little farther upstream is Hirschhorn, on a button-hook loop of the river, which is dominated by a glorious 13th-century monument to knighthood on the Neckar. Impregnable until gunpowder and artillery rendered spears and crossbows useless, Hirschhorn, like all other fortresses along the Burgenstrasse, was rebuilt over and over again. The present structure is a showplace of medieval architecture and fortifications with modern plumbing, kitchen, dining rooms, guest rooms and a museum.

Upstream past Eberbach, with its vast green lawns, fountains and flowers right down to the river, lies the tiny town of Zwingenberg, over which hovers one of the most magnificent of the Burgenstrasse castles.

Castle Zwingenberg is the residence of the Battenbergs, the German relatives of Britain's Prince Phillip, the Earl of Mountbatten. The family has opened a section of the sumptuously appointed interior to the public, but only three times a week from May through September. Tour hours are from 2 to 5 p.m. on Tuesdays, Fridays and Sundays.

Peaceful view of Dillsberg belies its turbulent past when armies laid siege to it.

A steep road leads up from the village and cars can't drive up.

Before you get to Zwingenberg, however, you can see the massive ruins of Castle Stolzeneck on the opposite bank. The fortress was probably destroyed in the Thirty Years' War and definitely isn't worth a detour. The same goes for the remains of the Minneburg castle, also on the left bank and just beyond Zwingenberg.

Upstream again a bit farther at Neckarzimmern the welcome mat beckons to swing left at the big sign "Schloss Goetz von Berlichingen," once the home of the famous Knight of the Iron Fist of the same name. Its common name is Hornberg Castle and it is described in detail elsewhere in this book.

The next castle town is Gundelsheim, over which the Castle of Horneck stands. Now an old folk's home, Horneck is not a tourists delight, even though it was once important as a city of the Order of Teutonic Knights.

Now it is time to cross the Neckar by bridge at Gundelsheim and to take the winding, paved lane near Neckarmuelbach and to drive up to the top of the

Neckarsteinach: Two of the four castles.

Burg Zwingenberg is the home of Battenbergs, relatives of Britain's Prince Phillip.

Knights of the Teutonic Order once rode across these ridges to Horneck Castle.

Bad Wimpfen . . . favorite of emperors.

mountain to Guttenberg, a mighty mass of masonry, still exhuding most of its ancient charm, to which has been added all modern comforts, including a fine restaurant. There is a museum there also and one may stroll throughout the dungeons and tunnels, along the parapets and in the turrets and towers.

Going upstream on the same bank you'll pass the decayed remains of Castle Ehrenberg, with only the square "Bergfried," the main tower, jutting up from the ruined ramparts. Overlooking the village of Heimsheim, Ehrenberg deteriorated early and little is known of its history. But there are some legends connected with it and they were fed anew when the 17-foot foundation walls were explored. In one bricked-up dungeon, human skeletons, chains and weapons were found.

If time permits, one should continue upstream to Bad Wimpfen, called the "Royal City" of the Burgenstrasse. Its delights include picturesque silhouettes of medieval battlements, the remains of the Imperial Palace, and a 9th-century fortress once owned by the bishop of Worms. This rascal fortified the palace and extracted tolls from all who strayed within his perimeter. It was here that the Schwabian emperors settled and built the magnificent palace which was often visited by Barbarossa and Frederick VII. The town was founded by the

Remarkably well-preserved Burg Guttenberg maintains its medieval atmosphere.

Romans and offers interesting evidence to all who visit there.

A recommended part of a leisurely walk through this medieval jewel of a town should be a climb up to the platform of the Blue Tower, the landmark of Bad Wimpfen.

After a fire gutted the tower in the mid-1800s, Der Blaue (The Blue One) received a new staircase and steeple, and the uppermost floor was remodeled to accommodate the living quarters of the keeper.

The keeper's family continues to live up in these lofty heights, and once you reach the top, a woman will pop out to collect 10 pfennigs for the magnificent view over the river and town.

HORNBERG AND JAGSTHAUSEN:
The Iron-Fisted Knight

Goetz von Berlichingen

. . . the iron-fisted knight.

Goetz purchased Hornberg Castle in 1517, and used it as a base for his raids.

HE WOULD HAVE been another run-of-the-mill knight if it hadn't been for three factors that turned him into one of Germany's medieval heroes: an epithet, an iron fist, and Johann Wolfgang von Goethe.

The first gave him a touch of notoriety, the second a fearsome right-hand punch, and the third a measure of dubious fame.

The fellow was Goetz von Berlichingen, the Knight of the Iron Fist, who died about 400 years ago, leaving a host of tales and legends about his feats.

Goetz' home country was along the Neckar River and the Hohenlohe area around Heilbronn.

The story of the steel-knuckled knight captured the imagination of Goethe as a young writer, and his play, "Goetz von Berlichingen," has since become a standard in German literature.

Goethe based it on the autobiography of Goetz which was first published in 1731 in Nuernberg. The play makes Berlichingen look like a Teutonic sort of Robin Hood, a champion of liberty and hero of the oppressed.

Actually, there's little historic evidence that Goetz was anything more than an armor-plated brawler who loved to mix it up, if only for the pure pleasure of it.

Naturally, Goethe's play had to include that famous line by Goetz allegedly uttered during the siege of Krautheim castle.

As told by Berlichingen in his memoirs, he and his men beleaguered the fortress and challenged the caretaker—one of Goetz's personal enemies, Max Stumpf—to come on out and fight.

Safely holed up behind the castle walls, Max gave them an insidious grin and politely declined the invitation. Whereupon the furious Berlichingen told Stumpf what he could do.

This was a considerably more earthy expression than Gen. Anthony C. McAuliffe's famous "Nuts" reply to a surrender demand during the Battle of the Bulge.

Taking plenty of literary license, Goethe in his play reversed the historic encounter, letting Stumpf do the beleaguering and putting Goetz in the castle. This gives Goetz a chance to

Reenactment of Goetz' defiant retort to besiegers of Jagsthausen.

utter his famous reply from a castle window. It never fails to bring down the house at the annual re-staging of the play at Jagsthausen.

As a tourist-conscious community, Krautheim couldn't resist that Goetz-given opportunity: the market square is graced by a marker which commemorates the event in granite.

And at his birthplace, the Jagsthausen castle, they sell a slim booklet which gives the Goetz exclamation in a few dozen languages.

They make less fuss over Berlichingen's iron hand, a marvel of medieval engineering, which is also on display at Jagsthausen.

The red-bearded knight lost his right hand at the age of 23 when he served in the Bavarian War of 1504. During the siege of Landshut, a cannonball smashed into his sword and drove it through the armor of his hand and arm.

Undismayed, Berlichingen designed an artificial hand and found a skilled armorer who made it for him.

There are three places in the state of Baden-Wuerttemberg which mark the main stations in Goetz's life—Hornberg castle on the Neckar, Jagsthausen, and the Schoental Monastery—all easily accessible from Heidelberg, Heilbronn or Wuerzburg.

You can start off with Hornberg, the magnificent remnants of Berlichingen's castle overlooking the vineyards of Neckarzimmern, a village on Route 34, about 16 miles northwest of Heilbronn.

The robber baron purchased the castle in 1517 for 6,500 florins—4,000 down and the rest later. The previous owner, Conz Schott, must have been a tough businessman because he tried to imprison Goetz when the latter came to Schweinfurt to pay off his debt.

Berlichingen lived there until his death in 1562 at the ripe age of 82, spending the last years in virtual confinement because of an imperial decree. As punishment for his warmongering activities, it deprived him of the use of a horse and

Drawing of the complex artificial hand the red-bearded Goetz designed for himself after a cannonball smashed his right arm. The device is on display at Jagsthausen.

sword and ordered him to stay in the Hornberg area.

Historians are unsure how he was able to write his memoirs, what with his artificial hand and virtual blindness. It is now believed that he probably dictated them.

But before it came to that, Berlichingen used Hornberg as the base for his forays against Swabian towns and led gangs of rebellious farmers against landowners, traveling merchants and nobility.

Documents dated 1184 mentioned Hornberg for the first time. It was conquered, destroyed and rebuilt numerous times and changed hands 23 times within five centuries.

(Ironically, the ruined fortress has been in the possession of the present owners, the Gemmingen family, for 300 years.)

Although the main buildings are destroyed, you can still scramble up the "Bergfried"—the tower—and enjoy the sweeping panorama of the Neckar valley.

In one of the tower chambers is a suit of armor reputed to have belonged to Hornberg's most famous owner.

The stable of the castle has been converted into a "weinstube" and restaurant where you can sit by the window, watch the river barges pass by, and sip a glass of "Hornberger Spaetlese," grown in the castle vineyards.

Your next stop on the Berlichingen tour should be the Goetzenburg, the castle at Jagsthausen where the knight was born in 1480 and where he spent his boyhood.

Go back to Route 34 and continue on toward Heilbronn. At Neckarsulm, take the Amorbach turnoff and follow the signs to Moeckmuehl.

In 1519, in the service of Count Ulrich of Wuerttemberg, Goetz commanded the defenders of Moeckmuehl castle against the forces of Emperor Maximilian. When food ran low, he had to give up and was imprisoned for three years in Heilbronn.

The castle is well-preserved, but is private property and not open to the public.

From Moeckmuehl, it's just a few miles to Jagsthausen along a well-marked road.

The Goetzenburg of Jagsthausen has remained the seat of the Berlichingen family, and is where the iron fist can be admired.

Every July and August, the castle courtyard serves as the authentic stage for the Berlichingen Festival, with Goethe's play the principal attraction.

The castle has been renovated many times (part of it serves now as a hotel), except for the north wing which has been left substantially as it looked during Goetz's times and which contains the museum with the iron hand.

For the final stop on your Berlichingen tour drive to the Schoental Monastery, 3.5 miles away.

When Goetz died at Hornberg in 1562, his family dispatched a four-horse hearse and brought the body to Schoental for burial.

The grave in the cloister archway is marked by a marble memorial that shows the knight kneeling before the cross.

A Latin inscription reads in part: "Goetz, the magnanimous hero, rests here in the depths of the grave. Among the honorable ones, his name was always mentioned. For with great valor, he fought bloody battles. . . ."

Suit of armor, reputedly Goetz', is displayed at the Hornberg Castle.

The controversial knight was buried in well-preserved Schoental Monastery (below).

HOHENLOHE:
Studded With Castles

Weibertreu women saved their husbands.

IT IS SAID that the basic philosophy of the Hohenlohers is reflected in their motto, "Auf Schwein reimt Wein, auf Wurst reimt Durst."

Roughly translated, that means "pork rhymes with wine, and sausage with thirst."

But it would be an injustice to the folks of this area, which makes up the largest chunk of northern Baden-Wuerttemberg, to reduce their accomplishments strictly to the level of food and drink.

For one thing, they've always known how to put a decent castle together, and that's why the Hohenlohe landscape is studded with them.

A long stretch of the Burgenstrasse, Germany's Castle Road, runs through the middle of the Hohenlohe.

Hohenlohe is the home country of a 900-year-old dynasty of the same name, which included knights, barons, dukes, counts and princes.

Present descendants of the once-mighty clan still own and administer some 20 castles, palaces, chateaux and m a n s i o n s scattered throughout the Hohenlohe country.

This is one of the few remaining areas in Germany where economic expansion hasn't crowded out ancient customs and traditions, where life is still dictated by the ebb and flow of the seasons.

In the crooked streets of its towns and hamlets the sight of oxcarts moving at snail's pace is nothing uncommon. And in at least one castle, at Stetten, the gate guard rings his bell every morning and evening, just as his predecessors did for hundreds of years.

For a healthy whiff of this Hohenlohe atmosphere, pick up Federal Route 39 at Heilbronn and follow it for four miles east to Weinsberg.

This town of 6,000, nestled around a vineyard-covered hill topped by the ruins of Castle Weibertreu, is proud of an incident that happened about 800 years ago and gave the castle its name.

Weibertreu, "Castle of the Loyal Wives," was besieged in 1140 by King Konrad III, and its defenders were on the verge of surrender.

At this point, Konrad agreed to let the women leave the crumbling fortress, taking along what they could carry on their backs.

The gals picked up their hubbies and carried them piggy-back through the gates. Konrad took it with regal composure and stuck by his word. His troops leveled the town, though, a fate that was to befall Weinsberg three more times in the following centuries. The last time came in the spring of 1945 when a 10-day artillery barrage rained down on Nazi defenders trying to prevent U.S. elements from crossing the Neckar.

Only picturesque ruins remain, but the view is enchanting and so are some of the tales connected with the fortress.

One of them originates from 1440 when a gang of "Raubritters" (robber barons) adapted the Trojan Horse trick. They smuggled a few of their men into the town hidden in a big wine barrel, capturing both Weinsberg and its castle.

Another of more recent vintage, happened in 1824 when the community raised funds for the restoration of Weinsberg Castle by mounting bits of castle mortar on rings and selling them.

To continue, drive to Oehringen, a quaint medieval town and once the site of a Roman garrison.

Municipal offices and a winery are to be found in the dilapidated Oehringen Schloss.

Oehringen's former Hohenlohe castle which faces the marketplace, has been sold to the city and houses municipal offices, as well as a winery. Although the castle is in poor repair, a visit to the huge vaulted wine cellars with rows of carved casks and barrels is well worth the trouble.

Virtually the same applies to the tiny village of Pfedelbach, less than a mile south of Oehringen, and likewise built around a dilapidated Hohenlohe castle.

The crumbling Renaissance structure fronts on a vintners' cooperative which processes the wine harvest of 14 communities in the district. The Pfedelbachers are especially proud of their 65,000-liter wine barrel (about 16,000 gallons), the second largest in Germany, so they say.

Two miles north of Oehringen, you can admire the Baroque exterior of Friedrichsruhe Castle sitting amid a well-kept park. The interior is not open to the public.

To continue on the Burgenstrasse, return to Oehringen and follow the road to Neuenstein.

Neuenstein Castle, a one-time water fortress dating back to the 12th century, has become the undisputed showpiece of the Hohenlohe abodes.

The sprawling structure incorporates a conglomeration of architectural styles —Gothic, Renaissance and Baroque—but manages to appear uncluttered.

Run by a Hohenlohe count, Neuenstein has been turned into a worthy receptacle for works of art, antiques, furniture, w e a p o n s, tapestries, etc., brought there from other Hohenlohe castles.

No one visiting the impressive interior these days would guess that Neuenstein, in the 18th century, was so deteriorated that it was used as a poorhouse, an

Undisputed showpiece of the Hohenlohe castles is Neuenstein, built in 12th century.

Carving decorates gate at Neuenstein.

orphanage and a hospital by the town. At one time, it was even turned into a flophouse where beggars and invalids could pick up a few pfennigs by working for a weaver.

After World War II, the present occupant, August Count zu Hohenlohe-Oehringen, decided to convert Neuenstein into a museum and gathered material for it from other family castles and the surrounding area.

One of the most interesting parts of the castle layout is the so-called Art and Rarity Chamber. It contains fancy knicknacks, intricate ivory carvings, bric-a-brac and such curiosities as the floppy hat of King Gustavus Adolphus of Sweden and a fist-sized bladder stone, allegedly the world's largest.

Among other things worth seeing is a huge 15th century kitchen and t h e

Knights' Hall, 130 feet long and graced by a beamed, unsupported ceiling of paintings which depict the Hohenlohe history.

For the final stop of t h e Hohenlohe tour, it is a 20-mile drive to Langenburg on the Jagst River. Langenburg Palace is the residence of another branch of the Hohenlohe dynasty, but parts of it have been open to the public since 1960.

The castle is best known for its beautiful Renaissance courtyard, but just as inviting to the weary castle tourist is an outdoor cafe on a broad terrace.

It's a fine place to sample the local culinary specialty called "Wibele," a baked concoction whipped up from beaten egg and vanilla.

Pfedelbachers are proud of this huge 16,000-gallon barrel in their castle.

Rennaissance courtyard at Langenburg Castle, a part of which is open to public.

LUDWIGSBURG:
Fairy Tales and Flowers

THE SPLENDID thing about the splendor of Ludwigsburg Castle is that it offers something for everyone in the family.

The opulence of 18th century Baroque architecture will be a joy to dad, while the missus will go wild over acres of flowers blooming in nearly every season of the year.

The kids may get a special treat visiting a smartly laid out fairy tale garden in which familiar characters come to life to awe and entertain the small fry.

The fairy tale figures, some familiar to American children but many of strictly European fame, are animated and wired for sound. Scattered throughout the sprawling grounds are giant toadstools which make good resting stools and permeate the Disneyland atmosphere with music.

The 250-year-old castle, once the residence of the king and the dukes of Wuerttemberg, is near the Neckar River in the northern Stuttgart satellite town of Ludwigsburg.

The written legends and recorded voices at the various displays are in German, but when the wicked witch calls out to ask who's eating her gingerbread house, kids of all nationalities know that Hansel and Gretel are in big trouble.

A multilingual green parrot of stone and a jolly green frog are the centers of interest at the magic walk, where treading on the stones of King Frog's pond draws a jet of water across at knee level.

Cinderella makes the scene as Aschenputtel feeding her flock of pigeons. After they're satisfied, they fly to their perch to await her next call.

A real live Forstmeister demonstrates his magic gun by pointing it at an eagle in the air. As he points the weapon, the electronically wise bird flaps its wings and presumably heads for safety.

In a picturebook castle near the real castle, Sleeping Beauty awaits her prince and the kiss that will give her happiness everlasting, while in the dungeons far below the giant Ruebezahl guards his treasure and warns away would-be intruders.

In a garden of red roses, the Red Shoes of ballet fame dance on and on through magnetic magic in their glass-enclosed ballroom.

But let's give dad his due now and head for the castle that could hardly be topped by any fairy tale structure.

Actually, Ludwigsburg Castle consists of 18 different wings with a total of 452 rooms.

The moving spirit behind all that mag-

Ludwigsburg Palace, built in 18th century, has flowers blooming much of the year.

Tinted gravel, shrubs and flowers make formal garden a colorful treat for the eyes.

nificence was Duke Eberhard Ludwig, a construction-crazy n o b l e m a n who spent 30 years planning, building and adding to his residence. It was finished the year he died, 1733.

The duke in 1703 ordered his court architect to plan a hunting castle in the style of a Roman villa. But when it was finished a year later, he commissioned a second architect to come up with annexes. Another architect, this time an Italian, was called to execute still other designs.

Eberhard Ludwig and his third architect, Donato Giuseppe Fresoni, didn't see eye to eye on many plans, with the result that the Italian eventually had to flee from the duke's wrath. His work was carried on by a more docile nephew.

This complex of structures — princes' halls, cavaliers' wings, hunting and play pavilions, art and family galleries, chapels, etc. — demanded a small army of painters, sculptors, cabinet-makers and other craftsmen to complete the extravagant interiors.

Flamingoes flash their dazzling plumage in the wide-open spaces behind the palace.

Children get a thrill when King Frog's stepping stones trigger streams of water.

The rulers that followed Eberhard Ludwig — especially Duke Karl Eugen and Wuerttemberg's first king, Friedrich I — added their own ideas to the place, but for the most part had the good sense to leave well enough alone.

A tour through the dazzling palace will leave a lasting impression of the high Baroque living enjoyed by the potentates of those days.

The same goes for the outdoor parts of Ludwigsburg: generous parks and gardens, imaginative fountains, even an aviary tucked in the hedges, everything related in elegance typically Baroque.

The geometrical pattern of 18th cen-

At the Gingerbread House (below), wicked witch calls out at Hansels and Gretels.

Magnetic magic keeps red shoes dancing while children keep asking how it's done.

tury royal gardens — playing with optical tricks and creating constantly changing perspectives — was revived here in the '50s for the 250th anniversary of Ludwigsburg. The entire project has become known as "Bluehendes Barock" —Blooming Baroque.

Some of the idiosyncracies of former Ludwigsburg rulers were left out, though. Friedrich I, for instance, used to have a hay wagon with stuffed horses parked permanently in the park. Whenever he yearned for some off-beat diversion, he took his guests to the wagon and pushed a button. The rear of the cart opened up, a staircase descended and there was a table inside already set for supper.

STUTTGART:
Three of a Kind

Schloss Solitude became a reveling place for nobility in the 18th century.

STUTTGART, former stamping grounds of the potentates of Wuerttemberg, offers a trilogy of delights.

Just outside of town is Schloss Solitude, a magnificent Rococo palace that crowns a wooded hilltop. In the center of the city near the old market place are the Altes Schloss and the Neues Schloss.

Solitude seems hardly the proper name for what was originally meant to be a weekend bungalow for Duke Carl Eugen, head of the royal house of Wuerttemberg, who chose the site while resting in the shade of five great oak trees after a stag hunt one day in 1763.

It became, rather, a royal reveling grounds for summer soirees and "relaxation" for high-ranking army officers and members of the court. Solitude became known throughout the duchy as the "Lustschloss," or pleasure palace.

Duke Carl Eugen designed the approach to his "hideaway" to feature two massive stone stairways with ornate balustrades leading to the airy rotunda which is the hub of the palace.

Chandeliers drip great clusters of crystal that gleams like diamond stalactites; ceilings swim in brilliant floral designs by French and Italian masters; walls are lined with Renaissance tapestries and colonnades and intricate Rococo frescoes.

Evidently the duke was not content

Duke Carl Eugen relaxed at Solitude but later established a military academy there.

with his creation. More architects were summoned, more buildings were added. Soon there were stables for a regiment of horses, officers quarters, kitchens, dining rooms, guest houses and a huge semicircular structure that was to become a military academy.

It was there in 1778 that Frederick von Schiller, German poet and dramatist, wrote "The Robbers," after Duke Carl Eugen drafted him into the military school and forced him to study law and medicine. Schiller graduated in medicine, became the duke's regimental surgeon, then wrote "The Robbers" in protest to royalty's infringement on human rights.

The second palace in the touristic trilogy is in the heart of the Old City near the market place and Schiller Square. Huddled in cloistered dignity from modern hustle, the Altes Schloss, rebuilt in 1553-1578, sits proudly upon the ruins of a fortified and moated 13th century castle.

Its courtyard is enclosed with graceful colonnades and three tiers of balconies from which ladies of the court tossed favors to the jousting knights and listened to the lutes and madrigals.

The castle now houses the Wuerttemberg State Museum and it is well worth a special visit.

Of particular interest are the charts which trace the development of man through the Ice, Stone and Bronze Ages.

The third in the Stuttgart trilogy is the Neues Schloss, a masterpiece of Baroque architecture built by French and Italian craftsmen between 1745 and 1806.

This was the winter palace of the Wuerttemberg dynasty, but it was virtually flattened during Allied air raids

Ladies of the court watched jousting from balconies of the Altes Schloss.

in World War II. Occupying two city blocks, the New Palace has been rebuilt at a cost of 31 million marks ($7.75 million).

Today the center section of the palace serves as a reception hall for the Baden-Wuerttemberg state government and as a show room for art exhibits. The wings of the new building, fitted with modern interiors, house state government offices.

The Wuerttemberg clan wintered at Neues Schloss, now used for state receptions.

LICHTENSTEIN:
The Duke Became a Caveman

Lichtenstein Castle occupies a formidable position on a rocky mountain top.

MOST TOURISTS exclaim in delight when they behold for the first time the fairy castle of Lichtenstein perkily ensconced on the Swabian Alb.

Schloss Lichtenstein, clinging to a pinnacle above Honau since the 13th century, was converted to a hunting lodge for the dukes of Wuerttemberg in 1802. It was originally a moated and fortified castle built by the knights of Lichtenstein, last of whom perished fighting the Turks in 1687.

Back in the old days there was nothing ornate about Lichtenstein castle. It was merely a royal protective device where the ruling dynasty and entourage could button-up against assaults by marauding hordes during the Middle Ages.

The castle was described by a Prof. Crusius of Tuebingen in 1580 as "a very strong-looking building which is located on top of a protruding rock, separated from the main cliff by a deep ditch. Since there is not much room at the top, the rooms in the lower part of the castle are hewn out of the living stone."

To storm the castle one would be compelled to scale a sheer cliff or span the moat.

Despite this, Lichtenstein w a s destroyed by the citizens of nearby Reutlingen in 1310, when tenant Count Eberhard II of Wuerttemberg defied the Swabian League of free cities and the emperor's army.

Just about the same thing happened in 1377 after the castle had been restored. This time Duke Ulrich II of Wuerttemberg was the hapless landlord. During the Battle of Reutlingen his opponents again clobbered the castle. Ulrich was banished from the kingdom and relieved of his dukedom. He sneaked back and took refuge in the Nebelhoehle (Fog Cave), one of the limestone caves in the area. He came out only at night, gained admittance by password to his loyal caretaker, and was fed secretly.

Many legends developed from the plight of Ulrich, and the subsequent Peasants War of 1524-26, during which Lichtenstein castle was beleaguered and beaten to its stony knees again.

Based on the legends, German author Wilhelm Hoff wrote a romantic novel called "Lichtenstein" in 1826, during the period in which King Wilhelm of Wuerttemberg was ruler. Stimulated by the saga, Wilhelm's cousin Duke Wilhelm

Death masks of famous European warriors and poets are in a museum room.

Richly decorated drinking vessel once belonged to King Ludwig I of Bavaria.

of Wuerttemberg bought the place to create what he called "a German knight's castle in the style and beauty of medieval times."

Completed in 1842, the old duke furnished it with fine works of art.

After Duke Wilhelm's death in 1869 his oldest son, Duke W i l h e l m von Urach, count of Wuerttemberg, took over, adding his personal treasures and maintaining the atmosphere of the old duke's dreams.

Today Lichtenstein is the family seat of what is left of the long and ancient line of Wuerttemberg royalty. The descendants live there and accept visitors who wish to visit and peek into the past.

Tourists may take a conducted tour of the premises (in English). Noteworthy are the displays of arms and armor, rooms carved right out of the mountains, works of art by Wohlgemut, Holbein and Schoen, death masks of Napoleon, Schiller and Goethe, and candlesticks from the czar of Russia.

Duke Ulrich II, the hero of many legends, is believed to have hidden in these caves.

HOHENZOLLERN:
Home of Emperors

HOHENZOLLERN CASTLE offers a challenge to make any red-blooded modern knight of the road put spurs to his supercharger and storm the gates.

The mighty fortified burg, its 18th-century restoration a faithful replica of medieval architecture, is about all that's left of the once-powerful dynasty which spawned kings of Prussia and emperors of Germany.

Exuding a plush hush that awes today's tourists, Hohenzollern occupies the high Swabian Alb peak in that part of a state of Baden-Wuerttemberg which belonged to the counts of Zollern way back in the 11th century.

From the nucleus of a tiny chapel dedicated to St. Michael in 1061, the castle grew. It wasn't long until a historian was describing it as "the strongest house on German lands."

To reach Hohenzollern Castle from Stuttgart, drive south on Route 27 to Tuebingen through Ofterdingen and on to Hechingen. Just south of Hechingen, on the road to Rottweil, is a sign which says "Hohenzollern 3 km."

A guide first takes visitors to the genealogical room, where the Zollern family tree climbs from the baseboard to the ceiling, branching out in all directions and showing how the descendants of the original counts split over political, religious and other differences.

The first completed fortified residence was mentioned in chronicles of 1267. The counts alternately fought each other, the emperor, the peasants and the Swabian League of Cities in quest of power and property.

Finally, in 1423, after a year-long siege conducted by the League of 18 Cities, the castle fell to a bombardment by catapults, and assaults by archers and swordsmen and was leveled to the ground.

In 1453, Emperor Frederick III ordered the castle rebuilt and from then on the Swabian branch of the Hohenzollerns grew so rich and powerful that they ruled as kings and emperors for the next 465 years.

But it wasn't all easy going. Lust for more power, vanities, jealousies and family squabbles continued to cut swaths through family ranks. These weak-

An inspiring sight — the spires of Hohenzollern Castle stabbing toward heaven.

Diamonds and pearls sparkle on the crown of Prussia in castle's museum.

Death masks of Frederick the Great (left), Frederick I are on display.

nesses proved disastrous during the Thirty Years War (1618-1648), when Hohenzollern holdings changed hands many times. The great castle became the property of Austria in 1667 and, for a hundred years, was all but abandoned, falling into a sad state of deterioration.

It wasn't until 1819 that the Prussian crown prince, who later became King Frederick William IV, and who was

Coat of arms appears on Swiss-made 16th century stained glass window.

known as the "romanticist on a king's throne," decided to restore the castle.

Redone in true medieval style in 1867 by the combined efforts of the greatest architects and artists of the times, Hohenzollern was no longer a drafty fortress—it had become a lovely palace.

Today's tourists at Hohenzollern will find a cozy restaurant there after they've given the royal roost the once-over.

And they will find that the vast medieval kitchen has been converted into a Schatzkammer (treasury) in which glass showcases display the glittering remnants of the once-fabulous dynasty.

The Prussian royal crown is there, along with a lot of jewelry and a few famous paintings, such as "The Petition," by Adolf Menzel, and "The Peep Show" by Nicholas Lancret.

The great halls and sitting rooms, bedrooms and libraries in other parts of the castle are dedicated to 18th and 19th century grandeur and contain a remarkable assortment of paintings, furniture, tapestries, porcelain, Swiss stained glass, paintings by Goethe's friend Philipp Hackert, portraits of the royal families by Antoine Pesne, who was court painter under Frederick the Great; and a large part of Edwin von Campe's collection of more than 300 contemporary portrait engravings of Frederick the Great from his early youth and his years as a great general and political genius to a graphic and pity-inducing sketch entitled "Frederick's Last Hours."

The last part of the castle to be visited before touring groups usually repair to the l i t t l e restaurant is the Protestant chapel, in which are displayed the velvet-draped, zinc-lined coffins containing the remains of the kings of Prussia, Frederick William I, and his grandson, Frederick the Great.

THE RIVER AND THE LAKE:
A Source, a Hero and a Tropic Isle

A CUSTOM at some jet set parties is to push or induce the guest to jump into the swimming pool.

At Donaueschingen Castle, this "modern" frolicking might be greeted with a tolerant "So what else is new?" For there, during the 17th century, pool-splashing tumbles were tops in recreation. The royal host often prodded fully-clothed visiting nobility to take a jump in the fountain.

Donaueschingen, at the southeastern fringes of the Black Forest, is the site of the splendid palace of the princes of Fuerstenberg, once among the most powerful royal families in Germany and still among the wealthiest.

The main attraction of their castle, in downtown Donaueschingen, is the spot in the park where the Danube River rises from a spring to begin its 1,775-mile journey to the Black Sea. It has been made to look like a fountain where visitors drop in coins for good luck.

Fountain in the Donaueschingen park is at source of the Danube River.

Nowadays, only kids jump into the Danube fountain—at night, to swipe the coins dropped in during daytime visiting hours.

But more about the castle: a few years ago its doors were thrown open to tourists because its upkeep assumed staggering proportions. Although the Fuerstenbergs spend most of their time on other estates, they still live there part of the year.

That's why the interior is a museum with a personal touch—among the fancy furniture, the paintings and the antiques are photographs and other family mementos, some of present clan members.

The present Donaueschingen Castle is relatively new, having been completely restyled by Count Egon IV from 1892 to 1896. He was a close friend of the last German emperor, Kaiser Wilhelm II, and the place is littered with mementos of the Prussian ruler.

Included is a photograph showing the kaiser in a pompous pose with a handwritten dedication, in English: "They say what they say. Let them say!" You figure it out.

En route to Lake Constance is Fortress Hohentwiel, built on a volcanic mountain 2,100 feet above sea level. It was never shaken by a tremor until the French came along in 1800 and blew it up. It took them five months to do it, though.

Hohentwiel, overlooking the city of Singen off the northwestern shores of Lake Constance, is a sad example of a castle that was impregnable until the technology of war became too sophisticated.

Archeologists have established the top of the Hohentwiel rock was used as a place of worship during prehistoric times, but documents didn't mention it until 806 when it was owned by Pippin, son of Charlemagne.

Hohentwiel changed hands from Emperor Heinrich to Count Berthold von Zaehringen to the Dukes of Swabia until it came into the possession of the Klingenberg clan, which kept it from 1273 to 1538.

But the citadel's days of glory didn't come until the 17th century when the dukes of Wuerttemberg were the owners.

In 1634, during the Thirty Years War,

Monument to Maj. Conrad Wiederhold (left) honors the man who beat off five sieges of Hohentwiel Fortress in 10 years. Footbridge leads into now-ruined castle.

the dukes appointed Maj. Conrad Wiederhold as fortress commander, and if there ever was a man who earned his medals it was him. In 10 years, Hohentweil was subjected to five separate sieges.

The armies of the emperor, of Bavaria and of Spain and Austria again and again tried to capture the strategic rock but were repelled by Wiederhold's defenders. Wiederhold's monument stands amid the ruins of this once-proud fortress as a testament to the courage of a military leader.

In the 18th century, the castle served as a state prison. On May 2, 1800, the fortress shuddered and bowed its head to modern warfare. What siege towers, lance and saber could not do, new French artillery could.

In October of that year, French occupation troops began blowing up the huge place and they kept at it until March 1801. There's still enough left, though, to give an impression of the gargantuan proportions of Fortress Hohentwiel.

Visitors may drive halfway up the hill from Singen, but they have to scramble up the rest of the way.

From Singen, it is only a few miles to Lake Constance and the island of Mainau. There's a Baroque castle of the Teutonic Knights there, owned by Count Lennart Bernadotte (nephew of the Swedish king). However, the isle is more famous for its tropical vegetation.

The Baroque castle on island of Mainau draws many tourists to its famous gardens.

SIGMARINGEN:
Pomp and Armor

BURG SIGMARINGEN was a soft touch—from one side.

From the north, Sigmaringen appears impregnable, squatting as it does on a sheer cliff over the infant Danube River.

Its south side, however, is on a level with the main street of the town of Sigmaringen from where it seems a kid on a bike could storm it.

To see for yourself, find Highway 27 south of Stuttgart, follow it until it intersects Highway 32 and follow this road southeastward to Sigmaringen.

Sigmaringen Castle looks impregnable from the precipitous cliff-sided north.

Dating from 1077, Sigmaringen changed tenants a number of times and was flattened by the Swedes in the Thirty Years War.

Today, the castle is in the possession of the Swabian branch of the Hohenzollerns, one of whom—Prince Frederick—makes it his residence.

Sigmaringen is important for a number of reasons. It houses one of the greatest collections of armor and weapons in Europe. Its collection of medieval musical instruments, gathered from all over Europe and Asia, includes wind and stringed instruments carried by foot soldiers as long ago as the Crusades.

Visitors can revel in the handiwork of architect Emanuel von Seidl, the Munich master designer who labored for 10 years to rebuild and properly refurbish into a palace the old castle which was almost completely destroyed by fire in 1893.

Its purple pomp is best enjoyed when one absorbs the richness of the Portuguese Gallery, the grand ballroom of late 19th century royalty, presided over by Neptune and a king-size fountain, hung with Flemish tapestries of the 15th century, lined with priceless plush chairs and lighted by cut-glass chandeliers. This ballroom is still used for concerts and occasional state banquets.

In the Hall of Ancestors, there are 26 portraits of the family counts and princes that give one a pretty good idea of what those bluebloods looked like. And in the Red Salon are 16th century Holbein portraits, including those of Charles I and Anna of Baden, who took over the place in 1534. Occupying other prominent niches on the walls are portraits of Emperor Charles V and Queen Isabella of Spain.

In the vast entrance hall of the castle is Venetian painter Giovanni Battista Tiepolo's "The Death of Saint Fidelis," martyr and patron of the royal household. There is also a 17th century French tapestry depicting the Holy Family in its flight into Egypt.

At the top of the stairway is perhaps one of the most valuable and intricately carved sets of furniture to be found anywhere. A chest and a sturdy writing table, gift of the Farnese Palace in Rome, are lavishly inlaid with hunting scenes carved in ivory.

Huge collection of armor and weapons is enough by itself to lure castle buffs.

Venetian mirrors dot the walls here and there throughout the palace, and much emphasis is placed on Chinese porcelain, hunting trophies, yawning fireplaces and elaborate Nuernberg tile stoves, which were needed in every room.

At the bottom of a flight of stone stairs is a drinking room, carved out of the rock which sports a 15th century fireplace and racks and racks of pewter and crockery.

Medieval musical instruments—some dating back to the Crusades—are an unusual display.

LAKE CONSTANCE:
Kingdoms by the Shore

THE CHARMS of Lake Constance have been appreciated by people as far back as the Dark Ages.

Prehistoric tribes put up dwellings on piles along the shore, the Romans fought sea battles with the unruly natives on the lake's wide waters and it soon became the focal point of important trade routes.

The lake's location between alpine peaks and the flatlands, favored by an unusually mild climate, gave birth to a number of small kingdoms, as attested to by the many castles and other regal haunts of past and present nobility found there.

A weekend tour along and near the German side of the Bodensee (Lake Constance in English)—the opposite side is Swiss and Austrian territory—could be launched from Lindau, known as the "Swabian Venice."

Sign points way to Waldburg Castle.

Lindau is perched on a small island connected to the mainland by a bridge.

The prevailing architecture is late Gothic and Baroque, and there are rows of houses once owned by wealthy burghers who tried to outdo each other in putting up splendidly decorated facades.

With the exception of the 13th-century Mang Tower (a former lighthouse), the Thieves Tower (14th century) and the Powder Tower (1508), you'll find no castles there. Those you can explore are at Waldburg and Wolfegg, a few miles to the north, both owned by the same family for several centuries.

Follow Routes 31 and 30 to Ravensburg and Weingarten and then look for the signs that take you to Wolfegg eastward through a peaceful countryside of orchards and farms. On the way to Ravensburg, you might stop briefly in Tettnang, once the residence of the counts of Montfort. Their biggest castle, the Neues Schloss built in 1755, today houses city and county offices.

The odd thing about palatial Wolfegg is its rural isolation. You wonder how royalty could stand it there for any length of time.

But they must have liked it, because the present Wolfegg Palace is the third on the same site. Two previous structures, dating from 1490 and 1583, burned to the ground. The second one was put to the torch on Dec. 28, 1646, by the Swedish troops of Field Marshal Wrangel who was repelled by his imperial opponent, Count Max Willibald of Waldburg, while trying to conquer the Lake Constance area.

Count Max began reconstruction shortly afterwards but, 40 years later, the job was still only half finished. Following generations of Wolfegg-Waldburgers continued the project.

A guided tour through the museum section (residence wings of the present owner, Count Johannes of Waldburg-Wolfegg, are off limits) reveals a wealth of art objects, antiques and weapons.

A unique feature of the huge Knight's Hall is an ancestors gallery of life-size statues representing 24 knights of the Waldburg-Wolfegg line, including Max Willibald.

The Rittersaal is one of the largest in Europe, measuring 170 by 46 feet,

Wolfegg Palace boasts one of Europe's largest Knights Halls—its 170 by 46 feet.

spacious enough to stage tournaments. The staircases leading up to it were built so as to permit horses to walk up.

Wolfegg is open daily the year around, from 9 a.m. to 12 noon and 1 to 5 p.m.

As you drive south from Wolfegg, watch for signs pointing to Schloss Waldburg, your next destination. Cars have to be left in the village and visitors have to puff up a narrow gravel path to the castle gate.

It's worth the effort, though, because this is a castle small and comfortable enough to enable you to picture a knight and his lady love living there. The caretaker and his wife make their home there and, for a small fee, they offer a tour of the medieval property.

The lords of Waldburg had their residence at the castle starting from the 11th century. Their days of glory came in the 13th century when they were made governors of Swabia by Emperor Frederick II.

The castle was rebuilt and renovated several times. The last major addition was a tower platform, added in the 19th century, from where a magnificent panorama of the alps can be enjoyed.

The castle's furnishings, weapons and paintings—most from the 17th and 18th century—were installed in the 1800s when the residence was converted into a museum.

Following this expedition to the hin-

Wolfegg's beautifully crafted iron gate.

Meersburg Castle, 1,200 years old, glowers down on the waters of Lake Constance.

Residence wing of Meersburg gives an idea of how life in a castle was.

terlands, let's return to the shores of Lake Constance where another castle, Meersburg, is on tap. A direct road leads there from Ravensburg.

Glowering over the placid lake, the fortress has reached the ripe old age of 1,200 years—still as grim and solid as the granite rock on which it stands.

Meersburg has undergone numerous onslaughts and survived them all. In 1334, Nicholas I of Kenzingen had 400 miners dig a secret subterranean passage to the lake while the castle was under siege by Emperor Louis the Bavarian.

The tunnel was completed in the 14th week of the siege. The defenders, by then in dire straights, were able to run in supplies right under the enemy noses and this forced Louis finally to give up the siege.

The entrance to the tunnel can still be seen as can the "Hole of Fear" dungeon into which prisoners were lowered and left to starve. Scribblings and drawings in the pit include a drawing dated 1527; a bit of advice, "Good companion, do stop grumbling if you want to alter your life", and a crude calender: a vertical line and 14 horizontal lines.

The residence wing gives a hint of always-rough, and sometimes-cruel, castle living. With its low ceilings, granite

Stylish Heiligenberg Castle is typical of 16th century German Rennaissance style.

floors and tiny windows, it is a cheerless place to the modern eye.

The next stop on this tour is Schloss Heiligenberg, seat of the powerful Fuerstenberg family which had large holdings in Germany and Austria. To get there, drive north along the lakeshore to Oberuhldingen and from there take the road leading to Salem and Heiligenberg.

Heiligenberg is a typical example of 16th century German Renaissance, a period when many medieval castles were converted into more comfortable, stylish residences.

The master builder for the Fuerstenbergs was Joerg Schwartzenberger of Landsberg and today's tourists are eas-

ily impressed by the range of his talents.

Heiligenberg's pride is a Knight's Hall (by Schwartzenberger) with a beautifully carved ceiling featuring 1,200 heads and figures. The ceiling design is repeated in the inlaid floor, the work of a local cabinetmaker.

The hall is lined with paintings of the Fuerstenberg ancestors going back uninterruptedly for 400 years. There also are two ornate limestone fireplaces, as well as cabinets displaying rare Bohemian glass and Chinese porcelain.

Another highlight of the castle is the court chapel with a deep-blue ceiling covered with richly colored ornaments. It was the last project of the castle's renovation.

ASCHAFFENBURG:
A Pink Palace

King-sized courtyard in Johannisburg Castle once was the scene of great jousting.

JOHANNISBURG, the pink sandstone palace at Aschaffenburg, Germany, sits alongside the Main River in restored regal tranquility belying its more-than-800-year struggle for existence.

What was once a drafty, fortified castle, built by Archbishop Adalbert of Mainz in the 12th century, is today a modern state museum graced with artistic treasures of the past.

Johannisburg was a weekend "bungalow" of nearly 400 rooms for a long line of rich and powerful archbishops and prince-electors, from Adalbert in 1121 to Archbishop von Dalberg in 1813.

Ancient documents, however, indicate

Clock (18th century) made of bronze.

that, after the palace chapel was built and dedicated to St. John the Baptist in 1285, a new tenant, Prince-Elector Heinrich III built the huge tower (it still stands) in 1337. At the end of the 14th century, Archbishop Johann II tacked another layer on top of it.

While medieval castles elsewhere in Germany were tumbling under waves of warfare along the Rhine and Mosel Rivers, Johannisburg continued to blossom as a warehouse of artistic treasures and as a show place for VIPs where royalty could relax between conquests.

But then came the Peasants' War (1524-26) and the uprising of the poor against their feudal bosses. During this shaky period, Johannisburg barely escaped destruction when it was stormed by the farmers under the belligerent knight, Goetz von Berlichingen, who championed their cause.

Goetz, he of the Iron Fist, who lost a hand in the siege of Landshut in 1504, overwhelmed the palace, at the time owned by Archbishop Albrecht von Brandenburg. Strangely enough, Goetz did little damage to Johannisburg.

In 1552, disaster struck. The palace and all its treasures went up in flames by order of a famous mercenary soldier named Count Albrecht Alcibiades of Brandenburg and Kulmbach.

The restored Johannisburg survived the Thirty Years War (1618-48), one of Europe's most destructive wars, even

Several museum rooms are devoted exclusively to models of ruins found in Rome.

though the castle was occupied alternately by the Swedes, Spanish, Italians and Belgians.

King Gustavus Adolphus of Sweden took over the place in 1631 "without a single stroke of a sword," according to records. Gustav resided there for a full year, so it must have been suitably appointed and reasonably comfortable.

In 1814, when Aschaffenburg was absorbed by Bavaria, it became the official residence of a young crown prince who later became King Ludwig I of Bavaria. The palace's emperors' apartment and rooms on the third floor are evidence of the pomp and circumstance of those days.

After World War I, restoration con-

Schoenbusch Hunting Lodge sparkles behind lagoon amid lovely gardens.

tinued on the palace and in 1932 the new art gallery, enhanced by a loaned collection of paintings from the Bavarian State Museum in Munich, was opened to the public.

The new interior of the palace is rich and sparkling with Italian marble and selected native woods. Art treasures include the works of masters of the Renaissance, from Hans von Aachen (1552-1615) to Januarius Zick (1730-97).

In other rooms, gold, silver and richly embroidered religious articles gleam from showcases; the library contains $1 million worth of bound writings, one printed in gold, another an original Gutenberg Bible, of which only 47 are known to exist; and some of Martin Luther's pamphlets, such as he nailed to the doors of churches during the Reformation (1505-1515).

As a companion piece to one's visit to Schloss Johannisburg, there is the royal hunting Schloesschen (little palace) across the river on the main road to Darmstadt. Called Schoenbusch (beautiful park), this regal retreat sits on a movie-setting lagoon in a vast English-style estate which is the last word in horticultural achievement.

Built by Prince-Elector Friedrich Karl von Erthal at the end of the 18th century, the small palace and park were his hideout. There is not much to see in the little palace except sparsely furnished rooms and lots of fireplaces where aristocratic guests gathered before and after the chase.

For sheer tranquility and idyllic grandeur, the baby schloss Schoenbusch is the perfect ending to a day of touring Johannisburg.

WEIKERSHEIM:
The Horsemen Rode to Dinner

TALK ABOUT the hardships of the Middle Ages: It used to be that horsemen could ride right up to the banquet table in Weikersheim Castle without so much as tripping over the threshold.

This was possible due to the foresight of Count Wolfgang von Hohenlohe, a comfort-loving man, who installed a gently sloped stairwell to the second-floor Knight's Hall which could be negotiated by man and nag alike.

Today's visitors to the regal premises have to leave their horseless carriages at the castle gate and pay for the privilege of prowling through the grounds.

But you're sure to get your money's worth because Weikersheim Castle has a lot more to offer than equestrian stairways.

The Franconian vineyard town of Weikersheim is one of the quaint spots along Germany's Romantic Road, which runs south from Wuerzburg to Fuessen, Bavaria, through some beautiful country.

From Wuerzburg, the most convenient way to get there is via Route 19 to Bernsfelden where you take the turnoff to Weikersheim. It's about a 30-mile drive.

The castle site, first mentioned in recorded history in 1156, fronts on the town's market square which is a travel agent's dream of what a German market square should look like—spouting fountain, timbered houses, friendly inns and all.

You leave these provincial trappings behind, though, once you walk through a succession of gates into the inner sanctum of the Schloss with its pompously appointed interiors.

The present layout of the 107-room Renaissance structure goes back to the above-mentioned Count Wolfgang who had it erected on the foundations of an earlier castle, beginning in 1586. Other Hohenlohe counts added more wings, and one of them, Karl Ludwig, put in a sumptuous, statuary-dotted Baroque garden in 1709.

Showpiece of the building is the Great Knight's Hall, an enormous 120-foot-long ballroom affair, which reputedly is one of the largest unpillared rooms in Germany.

The hall's ceiling consists of 69 paintings of hunting scenes set off by bulky stucco frames. The pictures are the work of Balthasar Katzenberger, who was hired for the job by Count Wolfgang and finished it, assembly-line fashion, in less than a year.

But what makes the cavernous two-story room different is a dazzling hodge-podge of stucco work, limestone carvings, murals and hunting trophies, much of it done by local talent.

An unusual feature is life-sized reproductions of animals — such as deer and elephants—with their heads looming into the room and bodies done in stucco bas relief.

Other furnishings of the hall include a bombastic fireplace and brass chandelier, and a reproduction of the clock on Strassburg Cathedral in France.

But the Knight's Hall is not only a museum. In the summer months, it

The formality of the castle garden is lightened by a drummer boy.

Lavishly decorated doorway has battle scene and limestone statues.

serves regularly as a concert hall for the young performers of the Jeunesse Musicale, an international youth organization devoted to music.

The other rooms of Weikersheim open to the public are kept in the style of the period in which they were first used. Many contain rich collections of antique furnishings, tapestries, works of art and weapons.

The three main gables of the castle look out to the Baroque garden laid out in rigid geometrical patterns and closed off by a so-called "Orangerie" in which the court gardener once tried to raise tropical fruit and plants.

Today, it serves only as a fancy architectural backdrop to a small army of statues — 71 to be exact.

In addition to Greek gods and goddesses, there is a cute collection of former castle employes like the court jester, the drummer boy, the brewer, etc.

Stucco heads project into Knights Hall.

COLMBERG AND ANSBACH:
Austerity and Luxury

CASTLES AND PALACES are much like the song about horses and carriages going together—you can't have one without the other.

You can, of course, see castles without seeing palaces but, if you do, you'll miss out on an essential part of life in those long-gone centuries of the Middle Ages.

There's a place where you can sample one of each in an easy day's outing. The palace is in Ansbach, Germany, and dates back to the 14th century when the counts of Nuernberg held sway in the area. The castle is Colmberg, a scant 10 miles away on the road to that favorite-of-tourists city, Rothenburg ob der Tauber.

Unpretentious, with a turret looking more like a silo than a battle tower, Colmberg dates back to the 12th century but is believed to be even older. It departed the control of nobility in 1880 when the powerful Seebold family purchased it.

In 1927, it was purchased by the late Dr. Arthur Voretzsch, a German envoy to Japan.

Voretzsch gave the castle an unusual Oriental flavor by adding numerous pieces of Japanese, Chinese, Indian and Korean origin.

Present owner of the old castle is Hans Unbehauen, an architect who plans to keep the castle open as a tourist attraction and to preserve the artifacts stored there for posterity. His home is just below the lip of the hill on which the castle is perched.

Colmberg is a fine example of 12th and 13th century castle architecture. It originally had a moat (the outline now

Ruling lords of Colmberg sat beneath this structure to hold court, settle disputes.

Baby bed of the last count of Ansbach.

barely discernible), outer and inner walls with heavy gates but no fortified gatehouse.

Never taken by storm (or so the legend goes), Colmberg survived the wars of the 15th century, a violent farmers' uprising in 1525 and the Thirty Years' War.

Hard against the yards-thick base of the turret is an interesting oddity of the Middle Ages: an outdoor courtroom where the ruling lord sat to pass judgment on criminals and to settle disputes of a civil nature.

The castle's library has fine leaded-glass windows, attesting to the fact that it once was a chapel.

Ansbach's palatial Residenz compares well with the austere Colmberg Castle because it dates back almost as far.

The counts of Nuernberg (house of Hohenzollern) came into possession of Ansbach in the year 1331 but it was not until Friedrich VI took over in 1397 that the first stone was laid on the site where the palace now stands. At that time, the count had a Wasserburg (moated fortress) erected which was finished in 1409.

By the close of the 15th century, the Wasserburg had been taken into the town of Ansbach, which had grown around it and, by 1637, had two towers as part of the city's defense system.

Ansbach Palace is a glorious blending of two styles of architecture. Markgraf Wilhelm Friedrich supervised (1703-1723) much of the construction and renovation but it was his successor Karl Wilhelm Friedrich under whom the bulk of the magnificent interior decorating was done.

Built in the grand tradition of Versailles, the Ansbach Palace is no hicktown affair. Bluebloods walking through this "house" could stroll through 523 rooms dispersed through four wings.

Twenty-seven rooms are currently

Picture gallery in the Ansbach Palace has some notable oils on its walls.

open to the public, including galleries with an impressive collection of art treasures.

First stop inside is the great banquet hall with ceiling frescoes by the Italian Carlo Carlone (1734). There are portraits of the counts of Ansbach there but furnishings are sparse — this was a room where balls were held and visiting VIPs received and so contained little permanent furniture.

To the left of this great hall is a picture gallery containing works of such artists as Johann Sperling, Johann de Pey, Jacob van Ruisdeal, Friedrich Naumann and Jan Vermeer.

There's also a dining room with walls covered principally by 2,800 pieces of glazed porcelain tiles made locally.

Some rich 17th century French tapestries are displayed in one of the ladies' rooms and throughout are beautiful chandeliers of crystal and porcelain. An 18th century porcelain chandelier, made in Meissen, was a gift of Frederick the Great to Count Alexander. Delicately ornate, it's one of the few from this period still in existence.

Most of the rooms are done in Rococo style and a visit here is equal to a course in 18th century design — to say nothing of palace life.

MESPELBRUNN:
A Moated Hideaway

WOULD YOU LIKE to "discover" a hidden fairytale castle and play knight for a day?

Schloss Mespelbrunn, an enchanted hideaway, and known as the "Pearl of the Spessart," can be discovered by taking the Frankfurt-Wuerzburg autobahn and turning off at the Rohrbrunn gas station onto Route 8, the back road between Aschaffenburg and Wuerzburg.

Swing south at Hessental and follow the signs up the valley to Mespelbrunn.

First-time visitors to this page from the past are immediately aware of the inevitable kiosks cluttered with postcards, souvenirs and ice-cream signs, the row of homey pensions and restaurants and the atmosphere of a mountain health resort. But the pleasant shock that lies beyond the leafy lane makes

Sleepy lagoon mirrors romantic tower and walls of moated Mespelbrunn Castle.

In the courtyard, you can almost hear the lonely cry of an imprisoned princess.

good conversation for years to come.

The eye-opener comes when one parks the family charger in the lot and proceeds on foot toward the wisps of mist that waft between the ancient willows.

There the invisible curtain parts and you are living in the past. You stand upon the bank of a sleepy lagoon which blossoms with snowy swans and is ringed with cultured flower beds, shrubs and footpaths—all surrounded by perfectly preserved 15th-century dwellings and stables and barns.

Across the lagoon, Schloss Mespelbrunn rises from the very waters in breathtaking medieval splendor.

You are no longer a tourist. You are a knight errant in shining armor. The hissing swans have become fire-breathing dragons. From the top window of the castle's majestic tower comes the song of a lonely, imprisoned princess waiting to be rescued.

Schloss Mespelbrunn, setting for German novels, plays and poems, was built on a pond in this hidden valley on a plot that was given by the Prince Bishop of Mainz to Knight Hamman Echter in 1427. Over the years the knight and his descendants built and rebuilt fortifications which, as they stand today, were completed in 1569.

Though the males of the Echter lineage died out in 1665, one of the descendants is still pretty well remembered in those parts. He was Prince Bishop Echter von Mespelbrunn (1545-1617) who founded Wuerzburg University and the city hospital.

Open to public perusal in the castle are the north wing, the chapel tower rooms festooned with period furniture, china and European porcelain, weapons and armor, tapestries and works of master painters.

The guidebook says the schloss is an "authentic German royal family museum."

The small portion of the castle which may not be visited is occupied by the present heirs and owners who are descendants of the imperial counts of Ingelheim and Mespelbrunn.

BAVARIAN SWABIA:
Frescoes and Angels

THE BROTHERS Grimm fairy tale, "The Seven Swabians," tells about a cowardly gang of dumb farmer boys who roam about looking for adventures, all of them timidly clinging to a monstrous spear. But the slightest sign of danger puts them to flight.

Ever since that story, the Swabians have been considered somewhat dimwitted by many other Germans.

Unjustly, it should be added. A tour of the castles of Bavarian Swabia—a fertile region roughly bounded by Augsburg, Noerdlingen, Memmingen and the lower alps—should convince most folks that the Swabians knew how to defend themselves. And they knew how to dish it out, too.

Our trip started out at Neuburg—just west of the autobahn at Ingolstadt—an ancient town on the Danube River nestled below and around the castle of the Wittelsbach clan.

Beautiful ceiling frescoes adorn "German Sistine Chapel" of the castle at Neuburg.

Neuburg got its name directly from the Roman conquerors who maintained a garrison there and called it Civitas Nova. But the city didn't get off its haunches, architecturally speaking, until the 16th century when Count Otto Heinrich built the three main wings of the castle, pouring so much money into the project that he practically ruined himself and his kingdom.

To add to his self-induced miseries, Otto Heinrich in 1542 adopted the Protestant faith and incurred the wrath of Emperor Karl V who took Neuburg from him. In his late years, the deposed ruler became an elector, settled in Heidelberg and constructed the famous Renaissance wing of the castle. He died there in 1559.

The most outstanding features of Otto Heinrich's Neuburg Castle are the exteriors and the arcades and wall decorations in the spacious courtyard. The structure contains Swabian archives and other offices and isn't open to the public.

But you shouldn't pass up the castle

Heavy knocker on the Neuburg gate.

Detail from 18th century stucco work in the lavishly decorated Leitheim Palace.

chapel (Hofkapelle), the oldest Protestant chapel in Bavaria.

It is known as "the German Sistine Chapel" because of the masterful ceiling frescoes depicting Old Testament scenes painted in 1543 by a Salzburg artist, Hans Bocksberger the Elder.

From Neuburg, you can follow the Danube upstream to Leitheim, about four miles northeast of Donauwoerth.

The mansion-like palace there was completed in 1685 by Abbot Elias Goetz as a retreat and sanatorium for ailing monks from the nearby Kaisheim Monastery. Small and outwardly unimpressive as it is, Leitheim has become known for the imaginative Baroque and Rococo stucco decorations of its interior and its gay ceiling frescoes.

Among the furnishings and other items on display are rare European and Chinese porcelain and a small silver crucifix allegedly worn by Mary, Queen of Scots, at the time of her beheading.

Guided tours of the palace, including the adjacent chapel, are available from 8 a.m. to 6 p.m. from Apr. 1 through Oct. 31.

When you return to Donauwoerth, you'll find yourself on the Romantic Road, that famous route which runs north-south through the length of Bavaria from Wuerzburg to Fuessen.

A connoisseur of medieval lore shouldn't pass through without visiting either Noerdlingen or Dinkelsbuehl, two medieval Romantic Road towns which are every bit as picturesque and not nearly as inundated by tourists as Rothenburg (also on the Romantic Road, 65 miles north).

Neither Noerdlingen nor Donauwoerth has castles to speak of, but both towns are still ringed by the walls, gates and towers that protected them during the Middle Ages.

Between them on Route 25 is Harburg with its towering fortress but more on that later.

The city map of Noerdlingen shows a rough circle, with the outer defenses strengthened by 15 gates and towers and with all main roads meeting in the market square in the center.

Just outside Noerdlingen is the site of the decisive Thirty Years War battle of 1634 in which the Swedes were soundly licked by the imperial forces, losing all of southern Germany.

Every stone in town fairly reeks of history and it is wise to get an English-language guide booklet at one of the local bookstores to dig a little deeper into Noerdlingen's medieval mysteries.

Virtually the same applies to Dinkelsbuehl, 27 miles to the north but outside of Swabia, which is famous for its annual Kinderzeche festival commemorating the year 1632 when the town's children saved the city from destruction by pleading with the commander of the marauding Swedes.

But Noerdlingen is the northernmost point on this tour, and we follow the Romantic Road back to Harburg, a one-street village on the Woernitz River towered over by one of the most massive fortresses in southern Germany.

Don't try to find a road leading up to the castle from the village. The only way to the top is by way of an access route which branches off Route 25 on the southern side of the castle hill.

Harburg is first mentioned in recorded history in 1150 and has been in the continuous possession of the counts of Oet-tingen since 1299. However, for all but 80 years, subordinates of the counts managed the fortress and sometimes the village too.

A guide will show you through the sprawling layout, which includes various torture facilities, such as a "heat chamber" (heated by flues from a large fireplace in the floor) and a cell not large enough to permit a man to stand, lie or sit down. However, most of the fiendish devices and furnishings were removed long ago.

Invaluable treasures such as manuscripts from the 8th through the 16th century, sacred items, jewelry and ivory carvings, tapestries, paintings and a library of 140,000 volumes are to be seen.

The pride of the collection is several wood sculptures by Germany's greatest 16th century sculptor, Tilman Riemenschneider, and the rarest piece is an 11th-century crucifix carved of ivory.

From Harburg, we continue on our

Harburg Castle's walls, towers lure tourists from the Romantic Road.

Swabian castle tour by going back to Donauwoerth and on to Hoechstaedt. The castle there, a squat affair with a tower on each of its four corners, was built in 1580 as a retirement haven for the widows of the counts of Lauingen.

Hoechstaedt's only mark on history was a 1704 battle in the Spanish War of Succession, won by the combined imperial and English troops (under the Princes Eugen and Marlborough) over the Franco-Bavarian troops.

The castle, half of its buildings condemned, is now a home for the aged and there's practically nothing there except the courtyard. Maps, battle plans and other mementoes of the 1704 conflict have been moved to a downtown museum.

Continuing south, one frequently runs into once-sumptuous castles and palaces which have been converted to 20th century usefulness by serving as city or county offices, schools, sanatoriums,

etc. Good examples are Dillingen, Lauingen and Guenzburg.

Just beyond Guenzburg, cross the Munich-Stuttgart autobahn and drive to Krumbach from where Route 300 leads to Babenhausen, site of one of the many castles built by the mighty Fugger merchants of Augsburg.

Babenhausen is still Fugger property and contains an interesting museum reflecting the fame and wealth of that mercantile empire. It is open daily from 10 a.m. to noon and from 2 to 5 p.m. On Sunday afternoons, it opens at 1 p.m. and closes at 6 p.m.

To wind up this tour, a trip to Ottobeuren, 26 miles away, is almost mandatory. Ottobeuren is not a castle, but a spa famed for its 1,200-year-old monastery with a impressive Baroque basilica.

The church was built in the first half of the 18th century and is considered an awe-inspiring example of German Baroque, a work of Johann Michael Fischer.

Pride of the Harburg art collection is this 11th century ivory crucifix.

WUERZBURG: A Feast for the Eyes

TO ART and architecture experts, the mention of Wuerzburg is inseparable from the names of two of the greatest German masters: Balthasar Neumann and Tilman Riemenschneider.

The castles, palaces and churches of the Franconian hub and the country around it tell more about the genius of these two men than any books or descriptions.

Neumann, Germany's best known architect of the Baroque, was born in Bohemia in 1687 and came to Wuerzburg as an 18-year-old apprentice in the building trade. When he died in 1753, he left a legacy of magnificent structures — palaces, houses, public buildings, bridges and more than 100 churches.

Riemenschneider, of course, was the dean of medieval carvers and sculptors, world-famous for his magnificent altars and statuary.

The memory of both artists is amply preserved in Wuerzburg, mainly at the Residenz downtown and the Marienberg Fortress looming above the city.

The Residenz, the home of the bishops of Wuerzburg, is probably the most elaborate palace built by Neumann. It is also the home of one of the world's largest paintings.

The horseshoe-shaped structure was

Riemenschneider likeness at Residenz.

One side of the huge ceiling painting which dominates the grand staircase.

built from 1719 to 1744 and its ornate splendor even impressed Napoleon, who called it "the finest Presbytery in the world."

One of its highlights is the mighty grand staircase of the main entrance, topped by a vault—60 by 150 feet—with the ceiling painting "Theater of the World" by the Venetian artist Giovanni Battista Tiepolo. It represents the four parts of the globe and the planets.

The palace's White Hall was done in white and light blue by another Italian, sculptor Antonio Bossi, in 1744.

Bossi and Tiepolo, the imported team of artists, did most of the interiors of the Residenz, but they were still under the supervision of Neumann, who commanded his army of painters, sculptors, carvers, gardeners and iron founders like a field marshal.

Every year in June, the candle-lit palace and its sumptuous gardens are the scene of the Wuerzburg Mozart Festival, a series of concerts performed before a backdrop of swinging Baroque.

The castle was heavily damaged by air raids in March 1945 but millions have been poured into its reconstruc-

Marienburg Fortress occupies a powerful hilltop position just outside of Wuerzburg.

Tilman Riemenschneider's stone Eve.

tion. There's also a museum, the M. V. Wagner Museum, with a collection of antique vases, prints and paintings.

The Residenz is open daily the year around, from 9 a.m. to 4:30 p.m.

Marienberg Castle is the history of Lower Franconia in microcosm. The fortress, which includes the Church of St. Mary and the Main-Franconian Museum, occupies a vineyard-surrounded hilltop with a rich 3,000-year-old history.

It has been gutted and rebuilt several times but always survived as a strategic landmark during the early tribal wars, the feuds of the Middle Ages, the Thirty Years War, Swedish occupation, French occupation under Napoleon, and bombardment by Prussian artillery in 1866.

Much of the castle, as well as the downtown Residenz, can be attributed to the Von Schoenborn family who, like the Medicis of Florence, were enthusiastic patrons of the arts and architecture.

Marienberg fell into disrepair in the late 19th and early 20th centuries, but a major restoration project was started in the 1930s. World War II bombings wiped out much of the progress, and rebuilding had to begin over again.

Since 1946, the castle arsenal and its

Wine Hall in lower level of the fortress has centuries-old presses, vats and kegs.

Echter Bastion have housed the Main-Franconian Museum with collections that pay tribute to the rich ecclesiastical and artistic past of Wuerzburg.

There is a sweeping range of paintings, sculptures and antiques through the golden Baroque and Rococo periods. But Wuerzburgers are most proud of the museum's sculptures and wood carvings by Franconia's most revered artist, Riemenschneider.

Riemenschneider was born about 1460 in the Harz Mountains and came to Wuerzburg when he was 23. His devout, inspired pieces — statuary, sepulchers and altar sections—are among the classics of late Gothic. His Altar of the Holy Blood, now in Rothenburg, is considered one of the most beautiful of its type in the world.

While Riemenschneider's preferred material was limewood, two of his most outstanding statues—life-size studies of Adam and Eve—in the museum's Riemenschneider Room are of stone.

Riemenschneider not only was highly esteemed for his creations, but was an able administrator who became an alderman and then mayor of Wuerzburg. Unfortunately, he became involved in the Peasants' War in 1525, was taken prisoner and tortured in the castle. Some reports say his hands were broken by his tormentors. He died in 1531.

Another impressive part of the castle museum is the enormous wine hall at the lower level, still equipped with huge wine presses, vats and barrels that were used for centuries.

Tours of the castle itself are from 9 a.m. to 5 p.m. from April through October, and from 10 a.m. to 1 p.m. and from 2 to 4 p.m. the rest of the year. The museum operates on the same hours, except that the summer schedule begins in March.

The third and last stop on this tour is Veitshoechheim Palace in a small village of the same name 4½ miles northwest of Wuerzburg on Highway 27. Maybe you'll want to leave your car in the city and go roundtrip by excursion boat on the Main.

Here is where the prince-bishops of Wuerzburg spent the summer months, enjoying the beauty of vast Rococo gardens dotted with beautiful ponds and ornate fountains.

Neumann was commissioned in 1721 by Prince-Bishop Johann Phillip Franz von Schoenborn to design and put in an artificial lake and, starting in 1749, he expanded the palace and installed one of his famous grand staircases.

The gardens are best known for their 200 pieces of statuary, most of them by Bamberg court sculptor Ferdinand Tietz. Since they were sculpted of soft limestone which deteriorated fast, most of the statues were removed in the 1920s and replaced by copies. The originals are in the Main-Franconian Museum in the Marienberg Fortress.

Veitshoechheim Palace's gardens are worth the short trip from Wuerzburg—especially for camera bugs during the summer months.

Vast gardens at the Veitshoechheim Palace are dotted with ornate fountains.

NUERNBERG:
An Imperial Fortress

DEFIANT TOWERS are the hallmark of Nuernberg, that German heartland city on the medieval trade route from the south.

Fortifications of the walled city still stand in great part and are among the city's leading tourist attractions.

The town walls, 3 miles in length, have an average height of 24 ft. and are slightly over a yard thick.

But the towers — there were once 128 ringing Nuernberg — stand out, symbolic of the city's former might. The five most massive of these contained the main town gates and were equipped with drawbridges to span the defensive moat.

Looming above all these elaborate fortifications is the Kaiserburg imperial castle, a solid complex of defensive walls and towers which must have been fearsome to behold in the days of lance and saber.

One of the biggest castle layouts in Germany — it measures well over 200 yards — the imperial castle is really not one fortification but two, or what's left of them.

Near the east end of the hill where the Bailiff's Gate stands is the Five-Cornered Tower, a gloomy structure which is all that's left of a castle originally built by the Salian kings in the first half of the 11th century.

The Salian castle fell at least three times in the 100 years after its construction in 1040 and eventually came into the hands of the Hohenzollerns, a family which was to rise to real power in Brandenburg rather than in Franconia.

On the other (west) side of the hill, the Hohenstaufen family built a fortress, partially to counterbalance the Salian castle, which had a way of coming into unfriendly hands.

No one knows what the original imperial castle looked like when it was finished sometime around 1150 but the heavy Sinwell Tower, the Heathen's Tower and part of the chapel to which it is connected are believed to date from that time.

It was Emperor Frederick Barbarossa who in 1190 enlarged and modified the palace and fortress walls more or less into their present shape.

In 1377, the city built the high Luginsland Tower east of the Hohenzollerns'

Towers of the powerful Kaiserburg loom over houses of the old section of town.

Knights Hall contains suits of armor, halberds and five big two-handed swords.

castle so as to be able to keep an eye on what went on there. A kind of "cold war" developed and the city gradually isolated the castle, erecting fortifications around it.

Hostilities broke out in 1388 and the town forces took the castle. Peace was made but it didn't last. In 1420, the castle was taken by surprise in a night attack and burned. In 1427, the quarrelsome Hohenzollerns sold the city their rights to the remains of the castle.

These were also, however, the castle's most glittering years. From 1050 to 1571, it was the residence of all acknowledged German kings and emperors.

Its most overwhelming sight is that of the Sinwell Tower in the courtyard at the eastern limits of the former Hohenstaufen property.

Built of rock-like ashlar bricks, dark-

The symbol of the Holy Roman Empire.

ened by age, the tower could be entered only by a foot-bridge half way up its sides, which are rounded, making it Nuernberg's only tower originally built in a round form.

Nearby is the well house, which probably dates to the 11th century. Don't miss the demonstration of its 165-ft. depth in which lighted candles are lowered to the bottom.

A rarity is the chapel, with its connected Heathen's Tower, completed under the orders of Emperor Barbarossa.

Members of the nobility attended services on the main floor where the altar is. Humbler members of the king's retinue were out of sight in a room below where they could hear what was going on through an opening in the floor above but couldn't see.

The peasants had to play things by ear in those days.

The palace part of the imperial castle was heavily damaged in World War II but has been largely restored.

The Ritter Saal (knight's room) has a ceiling of 30 oaken beams resting on an enormous timber supported by five central columns, also of oak.

It was in this hall that German emperors held their parliaments, with the emperor sitting at the portal where one enters the chapel.

Along the wall away from the windows are suits of armor, mostly from the 16th and 17th centuries.

The room next to the Knight's Hall is the Emperor's Room.

The reception room was where you waited (on work days) to see the king if he was busy in the Green Room, noted for its "four-seasons stove" and the big double-headed eagle of the Holy Roman Empire on the ceiling.

101

FRANCONIA: A Jewel Among the Forts

CASTLES and beautiful scenery are what you can expect in the Franconian Alps between Nuernberg and Bamberg.

One of the most picturesque regions of Germany, and one rich in romance and history, this area of gentle mountains was the home of the Franks, those feared warriors of Germany's early history.

A convenient spot to start a tour of this section of Franconia lies just north of the Wuerzburg-Nuernberg autobahn at Hoechstadt an der Aisch. About five miles north of Hoechstadt is Pommersfelden, a small town with a palace worthy of the highest nobility.

Stretching along a line eastward from Pommersfelden are a number of other interesting spots to visit. There's Forchheim with a history dating from the Frankish conquest of 600; Goessweinstein and Pottenstein, two towns with historic castles of their own; and just east of them the limestone caves famed for their stalagmites and stalactites.

Because of its beautiful state of preservation, the Weissenstein Palace at Pommersfelden is well worth a visit.

This monument in Baroque was built

Garden Room is a cool place in summer.

Weissenstein Palace at Pommersfelden has a truly stunning grand staircase.

by Lothar Franz von Schoenborn, prince-bishop of Mainz and Bamberg, who was also an elector and arch-chancellor of the Holy Roman Empire.

It took seven years—from 1711 to 1718—to complete this magnificent structure, which was used by the prince-bishops as a summer home and a hunting lodge.

Still the property of a count of Schoenborn, Dr. Friedrich-Karl von Schoenborn of Wiesental, the palace has extensive gardens and elaborate stables, the latter in a curving ornate structure opposite the main palace buildings. In the stables is a collection of horse-drawn sleds and wagons.

The main entrance to the palace is the so-called Treppenhaus (Grand Staircase), a fabulous creation in marble and statuary with a stunning ceiling 52 feet up.

On the ground floor, you'll want to see the Garden Room, a Baroque creation of stones, shells, urns, friezes, plaster and scroll work of fish, fruit and animals, statues of the four seasons and the four elements, and chandeliers.

One long wing of the palace is not open to the public, because it contains rooms still used by the count. The other, however, contains an art gallery with a collection of 700 paintings tracing the development of European painting from the 16th to the 18th century.

From Pommersfelden to Forchheim is less than an hour's drive. There you will want to stop for a visit to the fortress constructed by Bishop Otto the Holy (1102-1139) of Bamberg.

The high walls and sturdy battlements of the Forchheim fortification withstood three severe sieges of Swedish armies during the Thirty Years' War. Much was razed in the 19th century but what remains is well worth seeing.

Here also there's a museum containing a rich collection of artifacts and curios.

The scenery becomes more and more spectacular along the road east to Goessweinstein. It's hilly too and you already may be in second gear when you turn off Highway 470 at the marketplace.

Tours start at the lookout point at the northern end of the castle. A view of the valley 585 feet below and the convergence in the distance of four valleys may be had from here.

Construction on the castle began in 1071. Two centuries later, the castle passed into the hands of the bishops of Bamberg on orders of Emperor Friedrich Barbarossa.

Prince-Bishop Konrad von Schluesselberg was in residence at the castle in 1347 when it was attacked and besieged by a horde of Saxons. According to legend, when the water was gone and the food almost exhausted, the prince-bishop challenged the Saxon leader to a winner-take-all personal battle.

Primitive weapons used in the Peasants War are exhibited at Goessweinstein.

The Saxon chief lost the fight and was baptized by the victorious bishop. Out of gratitude for his people's delivery, the prince-bishop vowed to build a cathedral in the town.

Several times in succeeding generations, the castle was reduced to ruins and rebuilt. It did withstand a Swedish onslaught in the Thirty Years' War though.

There's a housekeeper's room with 17th century bedroom suite, some small salute cannon in the courtyard, and a wide assortment of weapons including battleaxes, suits of armor, swords, muzzleloaders, lances, chain mail and maces, most of it hanging on the walls of the hallway and in a stairway.

The jewel of the castle is its chapel which has a 16th-century Gothic altar with wooden figures carved by pupils of Tilman Riemenschneider. The patron saint of the castle, the dragon-killing St. George, is represented by an altar carving and a wall fresco.

A short jaunt down the road is Pottenstein with its castle on the hill above town.

Another imperial stronghold, it too was once owned by the bishops of Bamberg. One of the most famous inhabitants in its 1,000-year history was Holy Elizabeth, daughter of a Hungarian king who lived there in 1227. Her exemplary life and care of the poor earned her sainthood.

Goessweinstein's m u s t y atmosphere.

BAMBERG:
A Palace and an Egg in Your Bear

BAMBERG OFFERS the castle buff an ill-fated medieval castle just outside of town and a "youngster" of a palace right in the city.

Construction of the New Residence in Bamberg started just after the turn of the 18th century at the behest of Prince-Bishop Lothar Franz von Schoenborn, a man of the arts who also built the lovely palace at Pommersfelden.

The Altenburg castle, on the other hand, has a history running back to the eighth or ninth century. At that time, it was not a first-rate fortification by any means and did not acquire the stature of a castle, in print or in fact, until the 13th century.

The fortunes of the castle waxed and waned over the years. Strong walls and the rounded keep (tower) were put up following the end of the War of Succession in 1260 and by the end of the 1400s all was war-ready again.

The Alte Hofhaltung across the street from the New Residence in Bamberg.

Then along came Count Albrecht Alcibiades of Brandenburg-Kulmbach in 1525, who arrayed his host around the massive walls and so frightened the defenders in a few preliminary attacks that they gave up after only a token struggle.

Alcibiades is said to have hauled away 400 wagons loaded with silver dishes, money and other treasure. Eighteen years later, the vengeful count put the torch to the castle.

Altenburg was rebuilt but more bad luck was on the way. In 1719, lightning hit the tower and destroyed the top section. It was rebuilt. In 1780, a landslide carried away a huge section of the northeast walls. Ten years later, the tower caught fire and all the woodwork burned.

The castle was in ruins until the mid-19th century. Restoration continues under the direction of an association devoted solely to this purpose.

Only a mile from the Bamberg cathedral (as the crow flies), Altenburg is reached by a road which winds through the old part of town to a parking lot just outside the west gate of the castle.

Just inside the gatehouse and to the right you'll find a tiny chapel with a gravestone in its south wall done in the workshop of Tilman Riemenschneider in 1505. On the opposite wall are three other examples of 16th-century tombstone carving.

The tower behind the gatehouse is considerably more than 100 feet high and provides a fine vantage point. In a pit a few yards from the tower is a big, brown bear kept for the amusement of visitors. The bear is trained to sit up and beg for raw eggs.

If you're looking for suits of armor and other curios of the Middle Ages, however, you'll have to look elsewhere. All of the medieval paraphernalia which once was kept here was removed after World War II. A few cannon are standing about but that's all.

Such is not the case with the lavish New Residence on the Domplatz (Cathedral Square) in downtown Bamberg.

There you'll find rooms with many of their original furnishings, many oil paintings in the galleries and on the walls of most of the palace rooms, and

Gorgeous Emperor's Hall pays homage to 16 monarchs of the Holy Roman Empire.

furniture from a cross-section of periods in German history.

The New Residence was the fourth and last of those put up by the powerful prince-bishops who once exercised great political power in Germany. The secularization of 1803 was what dropped the curtain on this palace and many others.

This development was in the cards when Prince-Bishop Lothar Franz von Schoenborn started construction of the New Residence just after the turn of

The Altenburg bear likes raw eggs.

the 18th century. Thus the palace was used for a princely residence less than 100 years.

The lush interior was not completed until 1709, although much work was done after the palace had been occupied.

Designed by architect Johann Leonhardt Dientzenhofers, the palace wings form an irregular S when seen from the air.

Napoleon signed his declaration of war against Prussia in the New Residence on Oct. 5, 1806. The inlaid rosewood desk on which he signed it may still be seen.

The big festival hall, today called the Kaisersaal, is hung with the portraits of 16 emperors of the Holy Roman Empire, 15 of them Hapsburgs. It also has an enormous ceiling fresco done in 1707-1709 by Melchior Steidl of Innsbruck, Austria.

Other attractions are a 245-year-old French clock, which still keeps good time, in the bishops' audience room and a Chinese room done in rich brown shades with lots of gilding. Sixteen rooms are open to the public.

Some guidebooks also list a Concordia Palace to visit in Bamberg but don't be misled. It now contains classrooms and laboratories and is not open to the public.

COBURG:
Mighty Medieval Bastion

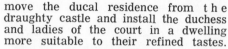

MARTIN LUTHER slept there. So did Queen Victoria and other assorted royalty over the 900-year history of the Veste Coburg, one of Germany's mightiest medieval castles.

Another long list of the famous may be appended when one adds the Ehrenburg Palace, a spacious residence built by the dukes of Coburg at the foot of the mountain on which their fortress rears like a stone Goliath.

Rich in history, legend and romance, Coburg offers the castle connoisseur a concentrated sample of palace life and castle living.

Like many another lord, Duke Johann Ernst longed for the comforts of Versailles-like lodgings.

He called a conference in 1543 at which the first plans were laid to re-

The mighty Veste Coburg was among Germany's most powerful fortresses.

move the ducal residence from t h e draughty castle and install the duchess and ladies of the court in a dwelling more suitable to their refined tastes.

But the Veste Coburg was no mean place to live despite the duke's desire to build a pleasure dome in the city. It has spacious courtyards and a complex of roomy, well-furnished buildings.

Dating back to an uncertain time — probably the 8th century — the Veste Coburg first is found in recorded history in 1056, when it was turned over to the archbishop of Cologne by King Richeza of Poland.

The castle passed through various hands (and wars) down through the years. Today, it belongs to the family of Duke Carl Eduard von Sachsen-Coburg and Gotha, a nephew of England's Queen Victoria. Victoria's consort, Albert, was of the House of Coburg.

Portraits of Victoria and Albert may be viewed in a guest room of the Fuerstenbau (Prince's Wing), a lofty half-timbered structure facing the main portal. It's the first stop on a tour of the castle.

Part-way up the hill to the Veste, you'll pass a hotel-restaurant (no refreshments are available in the castle). As you draw closer, the walls and battlements with their precipice of a defensive ditch will leave you wondering how men could dare attack such a lofty (it looms more than 500 feet over the city of Coburg) and massive fortification

Some succeeded; m o s t did not. Hordes swarmed around the walls during the vicious Peasants War in 1525 but they might as well have been throwing rocks. However, the need for stronger bastions was realized and these were completed by outbreak of the Thirty Years' War in 1618.

Duke Johann Casimir tried to keep Coburg neutral in that religious war but his sympathy for the Protestant side eventually drew him into the conflict.

A Catholic army under Gen. Albrecht von Wallenstein of Bohemia, and Maximilian of Bavaria, which was to go on to win some resounding victories, laid siege to the castle in September 1632.

Inside the Veste, 450 dragoons and

200 foot soldiers looked down their rifle and cannon barrels at the attackers and made things so hot for them that Wallenstein gave up the siege after only six days.

Wallenstein's path led to Luetzen where he was badly beaten, but the opposing Swedish army lost its aggressive leader, King Gustavus II.

Another army laid siege to the Veste Coburg in 1634 and the garrison capitulated after five months.

The stone bridge which one crosses to enter the main gate of the fortress was built 200 years after the last attack on the castle. Walk on under the fearsome spiked drop gate and you come above ground facing the Prince's Wing.

Inside, there are 15 rooms open to the public for a nominal admittance fee. In the Knight's Hall is a collection of helmets, weapons, stone and metal cannonballs, blunderbusses, helmets and other curiosities. Adjoining is the chapel, built in 1530, where Luther prayed during his months in hiding here.

Upper floors contain fine pieces of antique furniture, many inlaid with gold and silver; hunting trophies and oil paintings, which are seen by 70,000 tourists each year.

Famous portrait of Martin Luther was painted by Lucas Cranach the Younger.

Coach House has Baroque sleds with spears used for spearing rings in winter games.

For the ladies, there's the Duchess' Room, kept as it was when nobility lived there. Art lovers will appreciate a rare collection of paintings by Lucas Cranach (1472-1553), a friend of Luther who has been called "the painter of the Reformation."

West of the Prince's Wing, other structures surround a large courtyard and it is in these that another important part of the Veste Coburg's treasure is kept. Tourists have to pay again to see this Kunstsammlung (collection of art), but it's well worth it.

Tours go through the Luther rooms —where the famed Protestant lived, worked and relaxed in secrecy from April to October 1530. Luther was given refuge while his case was being discussed at a great council in Augsburg.

Not only is there a wide assortment of jousting and fighting armor in the Veste collection, but there are also dummy horses outfitted with full armor plating. One of them is mounted by a "knight" wearing a full suit of armor, and holding a long lance.

Other rooms contain major collections of glass, porcelain and wood carvings, including some Baroque masterpieces.

Two more stops will finish your visit. The first is the Coach House where there are two rickety marriage coaches which are among the oldest wheeled coaches in Europe. They're hand-carved, gilded, date back to the 16th century and were built before the principles of springing were known.

In the armory upstairs, among an assortment of scores of 17th century infantry rifles are dozens of ponderous defensive "rifles" with 6-ft. barrels, looking more like small cannon than anything else.

But the stars of the armory show are the two "death organs," multiple barrel weapons (one has 22) for defense against mass attacks. Awkward, perhaps, but the closest thing to a machine gun before the Gatling gun.

On the way down the hill from the Veste, before you've even had a chance to digest all you've seen, the elegant facade of the Ehrenburg will come into view through the trees.

Tired of castle life, Duke Johann Ernst moved the ducal residence into the palace in 1547, three years before the side wings were completed but just in time for a visit by Emperor Karl V.

This visit of the emperor is believed to be the reason the palace is called Ehrenburg, "ehren" meaning honor in German.

"Death Organ" of 1663 in castle's armory was nearest to a machine gun of its day.

When the dukes of Coburg decided castle life was too rough, they built Ehrenburg.

Until 1918, the dukes of Coburg were in residence here. Now, 25 rooms are preserved as they were and the rest are used for official offices and a public library.

As did the fortress on the hill, the palace suffered in the Thirty Years' War, being occupied by troops who forced the Veste to capitulate. Further damage was done by a fire in 1690 in which two wings were reduced to ashes.

The palace was rebuilt and remains in roughly the 17th century form of reconstruction.

A mixture of Renaissance, late Gothic and Rococo architecture, the Ehren-burg offers some fine frescoes and stucco work, particularly in the Riesensaal (great hall) a splendid example of lavish Baroque decorating.

A series of rooms in this same wing were once reserved for the use of Queen Victoria when she and her consort, Albert, visited Coburg. Reception rooms, guest rooms, the queen's bedroom (a painting of Windsor Castle hangs over the bed), a music room and dressing room were all there for her use.

The queen's dressing room, incidentally, was made with built-in wall closets—an idea which still hasn't caught on in Germany.

KRONACH:
The Women Saved the Day

BITTER ENEMIES, wars and women who saved the day are part of the story of a castle outside the main stream of tourists.

Lying close to the Iron Curtain border east of Coburg, Kronach's Rosenberg Castle does not enjoy the flow of visitors it likely would attract if it were not off in a corner of West Germany.

Kronach was an outpost of Catholicism in a nest of Protestantism. The property of the bishops of Bamberg, it was precariously situated between Kulmbach, Coburg and Lauenstein — all strongholds of supporters of Martin Luther.

Religious troubles first reared their head in 1430 when the Hussites (followers of Johannes Huss, a Czech forerunner of Luther) attacked the city of Kronach and laid waste to the countryside. They were beaten off.

During the Peasants' War of 1524-25, Kronach's city fathers and citizens council threw in with the contentious peasants and allowed them to occupy the city and the Rosenberg castle above.

When Bishop Weigand von Redwitz regained control of his castle, he levied heavy fines on the citizenry to penalize them for their treasonous conduct.

Markgraf (Count) Albrecht Alcibiades watched the proceedings from his fortress in nearby Kulmbach. The bishop's ways irked him immensely but he bided his time until 1552 when he signed a pact with France which the bishop declined to enter.

Alcibiades went to war and his men burned and looted most of the villages around Kronach belonging to the bishop.

Two years later, friends of the bishop helped drive Alcibiades into refuge at Schweinfurt, which was laid under siege. The fractious count escaped to France

View into the inner courtyard at Rosenberg Castle where 100 families are living.

but his adherents chalked up another mark against Kronach.

When the Thirty Years' War broke out, Kronach's Rosenberg garrison was reinforced and t h e bastions strengthened. The war was 14 years old when the Swedes under Gustavus Adophus appeared before Kronach Castle and the walled city beneath.

And who was with them? Why the bishop's neighbors from Kulmbach and Lauenstein, both liege to Count Christian of Bayreuth.

From May to June, 1632, an army hounded the city and the castle, peppering it with fire and shot, and repeatedly storming the walls. The citizens of Kronach were so enraged at seeing their neighbors among the forces attacking them and ravaging their countryside that they plotted revenge.

When the siege lifted, they marched on Lauenstein and burned and looted villages in every direction around the castle.

The worst was yet to come for Kronach, however. In 1633 and 1634, the stalwart Kronachers underwent two more attacks, the latter so severe that Duke Bernhard's Sachsen-W e i m a r troops succeeded in breaching the city walls.

The women of the town are credited with saving Kronach. They rallied to the walls with tubs of hot tar and boiling water to pour on the attackers who fell back after suffering countless casualties.

In honor of the courage and determination of the town's women, each year a procession is held on the Sunday after Corpus Christi, with the women leading the way.

Tourists passing through Kronach are apt to miss the single street which turns up the hill off the main highway and leads to the old city with its cobblestone streets. But, to get to the Feste Rosenberg, you've got to find it.

Inside, there's a collection of 18th century targets made of wood and each bearing a different scene painted on its face. Marksmen practiced on these attractive targets and bullet holes attest to some good (and bad) shooting.

The museum rooms are moldy and dark and not well cared for. Paintings, armor, field cannon, halberds, muskets, furniture and various implements cry out for a good dusting.

The locksmiths' room is interesting for a large variety of ancient keys, locks, hinges and door handles. You can also

Collection of ancient locks and keys.

see a loom used hundreds of years ago, several curious spinning wheels and a working model of a sawmill once in operation near Kronach.

The carriage house contains a wooden-barreled cannon made in 1608, attached to a caisson; two 19th century bicycles; early pumping trucks for fighting fires; pottery, rotting canopy beds and cases of dusty relics.

Otherwise, the rooms of the Feste Rosenberg are occupied by an estimated 100 families—mostly refugees from Yugoslavia who moved in in 1945.

Targets in the 18th century were painted on wood. Note the bullet holes.

KULMBACH:
Ghosts and Tin Soldiers

MAYBE THE GHOST did it. Maybe it was bad luck or poor leadership. Whatever the cause, Plassenburg Castle was ill-fated for much of its 900-year history.

The ghost, of course, was none other than the "White Lady" of legend—an apparition that is said still to be haunting the dark corridors of the Kulmbach, Germany, castle.

The legends vary as to her name— Kunigunda, Katarina, Agnes, Beatrix— but all are in agreement that the young widow killed her two children for the love of a dashing young count of Nuernberg.

The count washed his hands of her and the lady died — by her own hand in one version and while walking on her knees as penance in another. She is supposed to have put a curse on the Hohenzollern f a m i l y with her dying breath and her apparition made it stick.

The Hohenzollerns went on to found a kingdom in Prussia during the years after the jilting of the White Lady.

Kulmbach's castle was to become the Hohenzollerns' mightiest outpost in this part of Germany after they were forced out of Nuernberg. It and the Zwernitz Castle at Sanspareil are within an easy day's drive of Bamberg or Bayreuth.

The histories of the two are closely related but Plassenburg played by far a more important role in chronicles of the Middle Ages.

It was recognized as a formidable fortress by the time Otto IV died in 1340 and the Hohenzollern Count Johann of Nuernberg bought the castle. It was at this time, that the White Lady is supposed to have invoked her curse.

When the Hussites brought their religious warfare from Czechoslovakia to Germany in the 15th century, the Plassenburg was bitterly attacked but managed to beat off several determined assaults.

Shortly before the turn of the 16th century, Count Friedrich IV reportedly saw the White Lady but it is not known whether this influenced his erratic behavior from then until about 1515 when his sons removed him from power.

His grandson, Albrecht Alcibiades, came to power in 1541 and proved to be an unsuccessful soldier of fortune, causing the family great misfortune. Although brought up a Protestant, he

Tin Figure Museum scene shows town of Kulmbach and castle under siege in 1553.

A Prussian corps—tin soldier variety—advances on French in big 1870 battle scene.

threw in his lot with the Catholic forces battling the tide of the Reformation in Franconia.

In 1553, however, when war started among the fractious counts in earnest, Albrecht aligned himself with the Protestants. The Catholic lords of Franconia, Bamberg and Wuerzburg, whose properties had been mostly put to the torch, joined with the powerful Nuernbergers to conquer Kulmbach.

Waves of fighting men swarmed over the walls of the Plassenburg and clubbed the garrison into submission. Three months later, the vengeful victors set fire to the castle (it burned for 14 days), poisoned the well and broke down the walls and bastions.

Although the damage was extensive, it did not mean the end of the Plassenburg. Count Georg Friedrich of Ansbach, an educated, able administrator, came to power and worked marvels.

Count Georg demanded, and got, damages of 175,000 florins from the lords of Nuernberg, Wuerzburg and Bamberg.

Emperor Ferdinand I sympathetically added 82,000 florins and the count called in Caspar Vischer, one of the most famous architects of his time, to restore the fortress.

Cannon were by now a part of war and sieges so Vischer thickened the walls and extended the fortifications.

The Thirty Years' War brought with it more destruction for the castle.

After the Thirty Years' War, not much was done to restore the Plassenburg or modernize its fortifications; but it managed to hold out for six weeks when the troops of Napoleon besieged it in 1806.

The Frenchmen razed the fortifications and blew up the "Hohe Bastey," the strong tower which once watched over the outer walls.

You can drive into the castle grounds and park in the lower courtyard.

It's a steep walk from there to the gate leading into the great tournament courtyard, called the Schoener Hof because of the beauty of its gracefully arched tiers of arcades opening above the courtyard.

The two levels provided fine vantage points for spectators at jousting tournaments and other competitions.

The design of this courtyard with its Romanesque vaulted arcades and ornate Italian frieze work is a masterpiece of the Middle Ages. It was built following the great destruction of the 16th century.

Be ready when you step into the Plassenburg to s p e n d at least several hours. The first stop is usually the Museum of Tin Figures, which alone is worth an hour or two, and you haven't even started to see the residence rooms, the w e a p o n s collection in the south

Italian frieze work decorates a striking triple tier of arcades at Plassenburg.

Round six-poster bed is one of the curiosities in the castle's south wing.

wing or the art gallery and natural science museum in the north wing.

The tin figures fill about a dozen large rooms. At eye level, you can look through glass at hundreds of scenes peopled with tiny tin figures, perfectly proportioned, painted and placed with extreme care.

Some depict big battles like the Prussian-French confrontation at Krefeld in 1758 and are made up with hundreds and hundreds of figures in layouts as large as 50 square feet.

Contributed by various persons and clubs, the displays cover an enormous range of subjects: riding to the hounds, medieval town scenes, cowboy and Indian b a t t l e s, prehistoric mammoth hunts, World War II battles, castle sieges and court scenes.

The south wing is noted for its large open fireplaces, tapestries, a six-poster round bed and a room full of old prints showing the various stages of growth and c h a n g e the Plassenburg experienced.

Burg Zwernitz, on the other hand, a castle in the tiny village of Sanspareil, southwest of Kulmbach, has little to offer in the way of treasures.

It was in Zwernitz Castle that Friedrich VI in 1430 held out against a long siege by the Hussites, who had plundered Kulmbach and many unprotected Franconian villages. Friedrich finally got rid of the Hussites by paying a large sum and thus extracting a peace treaty.

Founded in 1156, Zwernitz, like the Plassenburg, was the property of the counts of Orlamuende but changed hands a number of times. It was burned in 1554 and rebuilt.

It fared worse in the Thirty Years' War than the Plassenburg. Protestant troops from Bayreuth burned the castle rather than let it fall into the hands of the Catholics; but walls and parts of the tower still remain from the 12th century.

After the 17th century, Zwernitz was no longer of military significance.

The 130-foot tower (120 steps to the top) offers a fine view of the countryside.

Less than 100 yards away, the tourist will find an extravagant creation of the talented Countess Wilhelmine of Bayreuth. Stretching from the castle into the woods for more than a quarter of a mile are hundreds of interesting rock formations, long the object of romantic poets and writers.

Wilhelmine decided to make use of this beautiful but unusual area to build a country residence. It is believed that she got the idea for an oriental-looking building from reading "A Thousand and One Nights."

Most of the layout was finished in 1746-1747 and, with a few exceptions, still stands.

Take the children with you to visit this. They'll thoroughly enjoy a romp through the woods, delighting in exploring and discovering one of Germany's most unusual parks.

Countess Wilhelmine had this open-air theater built at her Sanspareil pleasure park.

FULDA:
Wedding Bells and Fire Engines

CASTLES THESE days are put to some novel uses but not many can top Fulda's versatile Municipal Castle.

There amid an aura of Baroque and Rococo splendor, young couples, among them many Americans, are united in the bonds of matrimony.

The castle — it's more a palace than a castle but there was a castle on the site long ago—has two rooms set aside for the Standesamt, the city office empowered to perform civil marriages.

The Mirror Room, a lavish, colorful assembly of mirrors, gilding, crystal and oil paintings, is the office of the official who performs the marriages.

The ceremonies are held in the adjoining Green Room. There's the usual long table at which the bride and groom sit facing the official (the equivalent of a justice of the peace) but the room's other furnishings put it in a class by itself.

Fine silk from Lyon, France, lines the walls, and paneling with lovely gilding gives the room an air of opulence and well-being.

This use is only temporary, officials say, and wedding ceremonies will be held elsewhere when other quarters are found.

Powerfully sculpted statuary guards main gates to the Municipal Palace.

Oxen once pulled this 17th century fire engine in the palace's museum.

Other palace rooms are used for various city offices which take up entire floors. More space is being taken up by exhibits and, on the ground floor, there's a museum of fire engines and equipment.

The beautiful Princes' Hall — once a reception room of splendid proportions —for years had a low ceiling to mask the gorgeous fresco above so as not to distract students who worked in five classrooms there.

The low ceiling is gone now (a 1944 bomb did the trick) but the room is used for meetings of the Fulda city council and hundreds of chairs fill the hall. Chamber concerts also are held there.

Crystal chandeliers have been wired for electricity and bulbs now burn in place of candles, creating striking effects.

But this modern use of an antique doesn't stop there.

The former Audience Room of the bishops serves as a conference and committee room.

Some rooms on the third floor contain museum curios, while other rooms are used for exhibitions.

The construction of this dignified palace, begun in the early 18th century, took nearly 50 years during which time three prince-abbots ruled.

Later elevated to the rank of prince-bishops, the churchmen were in residence until the secularization of 1802. The last was Prince-Bishop Adalbert von Harstall.

From the upper rooms, the tourist has a view of the old Baroque quarter of Fulda. Across the way rises the 18th-century cathedral containing the 9th-century tomb of St. Boniface, the man credited with Christianizing Germany.

Collections in the top-floor museum include muskets, artifacts from the days of the French occupation of Fulda, coins, stones and Roman relics.

From the terrace, one looks across a broad sweep of gardens and lawn to the Orangerie — so-called because it originally housed sub-tropical plants, notably orange trees which were able to grow unhindered by low ceilings.

This delicate building with its slender pilasters and high French windows is the perfect complement to the palace and the gardens between.

If you enjoy palaces in general and the Municipal Castle in particular, you'll also go for Adolphseck, about a mile out of Fulda on the road leading south.

Here's a palace with rooms looking as if people actually lived there. Unlike those palaces almost devoid of furniture, Adolphseck is chock full of carpets, couches, stuffed chairs and all the things people ordinarily associate with an occupied dwelling.

C l o s e d between November 1 and April 1, it gets its name from Prince-

The dazzling Baroque grand staircase.

Abbot Adolph von Dalberg who had it built as a summer residence. Construction began in 1730 but the abbot had passed away by the time it was finally finished in 1756.

In addition to the plush furnishings, this palace has a stunning Treppenhaus (Grand Staircase) of marble, statuary, stucco work and frescoes. And, like most 18th century palaces of its type, Adolphseck — called the state of Hesse's most beautiful Baroque palace — is a mixture of Rococo and Baroque.

Worthy of close inspection are the palace's collections of tapestries, paintings, porcelain, antiques and sculptures of Greek and Roman origin.

Adolphseck Palace has plush rooms where its easy to imagine lords, ladies at play.

BAYREUTH:
Princess With a Passion

SELDOM IN HISTORY will you find a woman who has left such a lasting mark as Countess Wilhelmine of Bayreuth.

She left an enduring mark in literature, music, art and in two noble structures which today are tourist attractions in Bayreuth rivaling the magnificent opera house and the Richard Wagner Playhouse.

The New Castle and the Eremitage (French for hermitage) — a palace of the first rank and a summer residence of splendid proportions — were not built by Wilhelmine but her influence may be strongly felt in both.

The palace was Wilhelmine's home from 1754 when it was completed until her death in 1759.

The Eremitage was her "place in the country" — a gift of her husband, Count Friedrich — a place for fresh air, sunshine, artistic inspiration, strolls in the meadows and under the trees and good conversation.

The sister of Prussia's Frederick the Great, the little princess brought a French esprit along with a Teutonic gusto to Bayreuth, transforming it into

Countess Wilhelmine imported a Roman ruin to use as her dog's tombstone.

a cultural oasis of 18th century Germany.

Wilhelmine was a many-sided and talented woman. She spoke fluent French, played four musical instruments, composed music, wrote plays and texts for operas, planned and worked in her gardens and was an amateur artist of considerable merit.

The old palace in Bayreuth burned in 1752 and Wilhelmine and her husband had a new one built in just two years. The dark-haired countess had many ideas for the new palace which were incorporated into the design by Joseph Saint-Pierre, the architect.

The new palace has 21 rooms open to the public in addition to a museum. It's right in town and easy to find.

In front of the less-than-impressive facade (it could use a good scrubbing) is a Baroque fountain of Count Christian Ernst in the act of trampling the Turks beneath the hooves of his horse.

Inside the palace, you will find parquet floors in every room and it's interesting to observe their changing patterns as you walk through.

It also excels in an extravant characteristic of Rococo — garden rooms — and there are seven of them. These rooms all adjoin the gardens and have many flowers, plants, and animals worked into lavish decorations so as to give the inhabitant the feeling of being "in nature" or in a strange exotic garden.

There are a number of tapestry rooms in the New Palace; most of the tapestries are 17th century works from Belgium. A curiosity is the Mirror Illusion Room with its fragmented pieces of reflecting surfaces which give the over-all impression of a ruin.

Typically Rococo, the mirror room has dragons, lions and dolphins playing among the mirrors.

The long Banquet Room is, perhaps, the most tasteful example of Rococo decorating you will find anywhere. The long table seats 26 persons. It's flanked by dark, highly polished wood paneling, which rises to the ceiling where gilded palm trees sway.

The ceiling swarms with gilded dragons and other legendary animals. Candelabras line the window wall. The total effect is daring but in extremely good taste.

Breezy Rococo decorations in the Italian wing brighten New Palace's garden rooms.

The Eremitage lies only a few miles east of Bayreuth, on the other side of the Autobahn, in a lovely wooded setting.

Originally built by one of the counts who preceded her husband, the Eremitage was a hunting lodge which Wilhelmina transformed into a palatial summer residence.

The rooms once opened individually on a central courtyard but Wilhelmine cut a hallway through and closed most of them off from the courtyard. She also had the rooms made over in a style to suit her cultivated taste and added a Rococo Japanese room and a music room. Wilhelmine spent many hours writing and working in these rooms.

Some of the plain, sparsely furnished monks' rooms of the hermitage (which gave the place its name) remain, too, for contrast.

A must when visiting the Eremitage is the grotto in the cellar across the courtyard from the entrance hall.

The grotto has numerous water spouts hidden in the pebbled floor, controlled by levers hidden from the view in a narrow side passageway. It is said that Count Friedrich amused himself by catching unsuspecting guests in his grotto and turning on the water.

There's also an impressive outdoor exhibition of water play at the adjacent pleasure palace built by Wilhelmine but it's not as much fun.

You'll find a half-dozen ruins scattered about in unlikely places.

Count Friedrich quenched his thirst for practical jokes in this grotto.

BURGHAUSEN:
The Longest of Them All

LONG, DARK and handsome—that's Burghausen Castle's claim to fame.

But be sure to accentuate the long, for this sprawling fortress lays undisputed claim to being the very longest in all of Germany.

It's just over a kilometer (more than a half-mile) from one end to the other.

There's more to Burghausen Castle than an entry in castle record books, however.

As near as the archeologists and historians can tell, the first battleaxe was hurled from this site in about the year 748 but the first proper fortification didn't appear until the 10th century.

The first royal court was established in Burghausen by Emperor Konrad II in 1025. For about a hundred years from that time, the flag of the counts of Burghausen—a red dragon on a silver field—fluttered over the castle.

This line expired in the 12th century and, like Burghausen's big brother to the north, Landshut, it came into the hands of the Wittelsbachs under a united Bavaria.

The town (same name—derived from the castle) of Burghausen is on the banks of the Salzach River, about 15

Gothic chapel was constructed in 1255.

Model of Burghausen Castle, Germany's longest, shows its complex of defenses.

miles upstream from Braunau, Austria, where a man by the name of Adolf Hitler was born.

A high ridge runs along the river with the town between them at this point. Like a long narrow peninsula ending in the sea, the steep-sided r i d g e ends abruptly as if some giant had taken a slice of birthday cake off the end.

The result is a position of great natural defense: the slopes of the ridge are steep; the river provides a natural barrier on the east; Lake Woehr shields most of the western side; and there are no nearby heights from which to base attacks with cannon or otherwise.

Burghausen Castle had one defensive flaw which could have (but didn't) doom it to the fate of Schloss Neuburg just south of Passau. Neuburg Castle also was easily approachable from the landward side. It was attacked 15 times and preserved its perfect record by succumbing each time.

The ridge at Burghausen, however, made the approach to the castle on its end limited to the width of the ridge. By the 13th century, the dukes of Lower Bavaria, who for 250 years stored their gold and valuables in this stronghold, got worried about this vulnerability from the north.

A complex of defensive walls integrated town and castle into a single solid defensive unit by 1387.

Tough a nut as this would have been to crack, it was made even tougher during the reign of Duke George the Wealthy (1479-1503).

Walls already prevented an easy approach from the north end of the ridge but, under George's direction, new drawbridges, dropgates, strongholds, moats and towers were constructed.

Anyone entertaining plans to attack would have had to assault four successive lines of defense in order to break through across level ground to the fearsome fortress-palace.

None of this looks so formidable today as you walk through the successive courtyards but bear in mind that no attacker ever succeeded in conquering Burghausen by storm.

To get the full impact of this sprawling layout, one would have to hover overhead in a helicopter.

The main palace building, which was started in 1140 and finished 300 years later, has a collection of 14th to 18th century paintings, mostly with religious themes, late Gothic furniture, tapestries and many wood-carvings.

Next door, in the Heimat Museum, there's more to excite the imagination.

Things like old Bavarian furniture, an 18th century house altar—most unusual with its carving of a crucified Christ lying under the altar—a couple of fire engines, post coach, wrought iron grave markers (a whole room full), the usual sabers, muskets and daggers, a display of medieval clothes, another of handicraft articles and a collection of stuffed birds.

Just south of Burghausen is the quiet market town of Tittmoning, which also has a castle worth visiting. For nearly 600 years, it was the summer residence of Salzburg's powerful archbishops.

Tittmoning Castle, built in 1234, was originally put up as a border fortress against the encroachments of the aggressive dukes of Bavaria. Taken by storm several times, it came into the hands of Bavaria once and for all in 1816.

Unprepossessing though it may appear from the outside, Tittmoning provides the visitor with a nice surprise. It has a well-preserved parapet ramp and a museum crammed with curios and artifacts well worth seeing.

Colorful Tittmoning porcelain oven.

LANDSHUT:
A Big Wedding Amid the Sieges

HARD LUCK has dogged Landshut's ancient castle and palace down through the centuries.

The battering ram ferocity of sieges and subjugation left their marks on the ragged stones of the lofty castle and on the frescoed walls of the downtown palace.

But the destruction didn't end with the last zing of a crossbow or the last plop of a Swedish cannonball.

In 1961, one whole wing of Trausnitz Castle, with its priceless Renaissance furnishings, went up in flames. A care-

Festival every three years commemorates a regal 15th century marriage.

lessly left-on hot water heater caused the fire in which the relics of nearly a thousand years were destroyed.

This piece of hard luck equaled that of the 17th century when the Swedes stomped into town during the Thirty Years War, looted the palace of its great treasures and stormed and ravaged the castle.

Landshut is a quiet city of about 50,000 population, some 60 miles northeast of Munich.

It wasn't always quiet.

Long before Munich rose to the top of the heap as Bavaria's capital city, Landshut was that state's No. 1 city. Situated on a crossroads of two important trade routes and at one of the best fords across the Isar River, Landshut's medieval importance is stressed every three years in a big festival.

The fest commemorates the wedding feast of the prince of Landshut in 1475 when Duke George the Wealthy married amid great splendor the beautiful Polish Princess Jadwiga.

Meanwhile, back at the castle, the caretaker is bemoaning the fact that so little remains to attract tourists to the foreboding structure with a history reaching back to 1180.

The road into the castle passes through an outer gate and under high ramparts maintained in remarkably good condition. A timbered bridge spans the deep moat once crossed only over a ponderous drawbridge; immediately inside is the ticket window and a glimpse of pure Renaissance architecture facing the courtyard.

To the left, is the ruined Fuerstenbau, now under restoration.

Untouched by the fire, which destroyed 25 rooms, was the castle's famous St. George's Chapel.

The main sight left at Burg Trausnitz is the view from the fourth-floor solarium. From there, where musicians once played for listening and dancing on warm summer evenings, the orange-red tiles of Landshut's roofs cast a warm glow in the air.

From the solarium (Soller in German) you can also view the Swede's Gate on the eastern end of the burg, so named because it was here that the Swedes under Gustavus Adolphus smashed their way into the castle during the Thirty Years War.

Trausnitz Castle existed before the town which grew up around its walls. Both originally were called Landshut—Hat of the Land—in deference to their mighty position as defenders of the countryside. It was sometime later that the castle got its present name.

The Wittelsbach family—still an important name in German aristocratic circles—founded the castle around the turn of the 13th century and made it the official residence of the dukes of Lower Bavaria.

When the last of the Landshut dukes, George, died in 1503 without an heir, a terrific battle broke out for possession of Lower Bavaria and his other holdings. Winner in the struggle was Duke Albrecht IV of Munich, who annexed the whole business into his own realm of Upper Bavaria.

From then on, Landshut's importance dwindled. Albrecht's brother, Duke Ludwig IX, was given charge of Lower Bavaria and he wrought many changes, most important of which was construction of the Landshut Residenz.

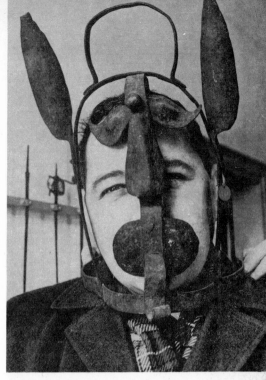

Mask "encouraged" prisoners to talk.

Woodcarving (16th century) stands in museum of the Landshut Residenz.

The result was the first Renaissance palace built on German soil.

Final work was completed in 1543. Scarcely two years later, Ludwig X was dead and with him went all the dreams for a revival of Landshut's importance.

Crowded in on three sides, the Landshut Residenz is scarcely noticeable in a street of quaint buildings, one much like the other. It fronts on the Laendstrasse across from the Gothic Rathaus.

Especially noteworthy are the palace's many lovely ceilings with lavish gilding and frescoes. Venus and Apollo rooms are certainly outstanding but the most extravagant of all is the big Italian ballroom.

There are models and drawings, treasure chests—16 or so in one room—suits of armor, 14th to 20th century rifles, torture masks, porcelain, furniture, medieval money, swords and other aggressive hardware.

Possibly the most famous pieces are the wood carvings done by Hans Leinberger in the early years of the 16th century. You may be interested too in looking at a portrait of the palace's builder, Ludwig X, as he looked at 36.

Ludwig, a confirmed bachelor, loved his wine, women and song. But the mileage shows.

THE ALTMUEHLTAL:
Germany's Old Mill Stream

THE ALTMUEHLTAL — that's the Valley of the Old Mill Stream to the uninitiated—has a lot going for it.

Not only are there scads of castles flung along its winding course through Franconia but it has a rich history reaching back to Roman times and beyond into the darkened recesses of prehistoric times.

Celts and Romans once defended hill where Pappenheim's ruins now stand.

In its 137-mile course from near Rothenburg until it empties into the Danube at Kelheim, the Altmuehl passes through some beautiful country. The section of the river valley running downstream from Pappenheim to the Danube certainly offers scenery on a par with any to be found in central Germany.

Castle buffs poking through this region will find plenty of moldering stones but most of them in castles of no enormous age. Battles and sieges involving them were, for the most part, during the Thirty Years War (1618-1648).

Starting at Pappenheim with its ruined schloss atop the mountain, a castle tour of this end of the valley continues to Eichstaett with its bishop-built fortress, past diverse ruins and privately owned castles like Schloss Rosenburg at Riedenburg and on to compact Burg Prunn and the impressive Befreiungshalle by Kelheim where some of Germany's greatest heroes are honored.

The castle at Pappenheim, now largely in ruins, was once one of the most powerful bastions in Bavaria. Its history goes back to the year 1050 but long before that the heights on which it was built provided refuge for Celts and, later, Romans.

Prints of the castle as it was before the 17th century show a proud, well-fortified fortress with high corner towers and a goodly number of outer walls and defenses. A high palace and other buildings once inside the walls are now gone.

Much of what was there was pounded to rubble during three sieges by the Swedes during the Thirty Years War. Twice they came in 1632 and, while the city fell, the castle held out under the determined leadership of a Captain Fink.

In 1633, the Swedes returned to Pappenheim, this time with many heavy cannon and an army of footsoldiers. Food and water were getting in short supply as the days went by and the piles of bodies beneath the walls grew higher.

Three days of concentrated pounding by Swedish artillery reduced the once-proud Pappenheimer Schloss to rubble.

Finally, Capt. Fink finked out. With resistance no longer possible, he sent his surrender to the Swedes, who graciously allowed the garrison to march away with packs and guns in recognition of their brave and spirited defense.

Drive east from Pappenheim along the Altmuehl and, just before hitting Eichstaett, you'll see the rather imposing Willibaldsburg standing tall and proud.

Eichstaett, like Pappenheim, was put to the torch by the Swedes.

Though Irish monks worked diligently to Christianize this part of Germany, it was under Bishop Willibald (700-787) that the greatest strides were made.

The first castle went up in 908 in response to the threat from raiding Hungarian tribes. Soon, the city was walled and the castle, in true medieval style, was linked into the defensive system.

Bishop Berthold von Zollern (1354-1365) was dissatisfied with the burg, however, and ordered the construction of the Willibaldsburg as a fortress and residence.

After the destruction of the 1630s, bishops rebuilt the old castle but gradually moved their residence to new quarters in the city.

The castle, while interesting from a romantic viewpoint, is possibly best known for the splendid little paleontological museum it contains. There, you can look upon the assembled bones of a mammoth found nearby in 1909, fossils of a 13-foot crocodile, snakes, fish, snails and other oddities (with names like pterodactylus and pleurosaurus in sur-

Willibaldsburg . . . bones and battles.

The castle at Eichstaett is well-known for its fine paleontological collection.

Many of Germany's greatest heroes are honored in Befreiungshalle near Kelheim.

prising numbers, among the Roman artifacts).

The castle and museum are open to tourists during the summer months from 9 to 12 noon and from 1 to 5 p.m. In the winter, hours are reduced to from 10 a.m. to 12 and from 2 to 4 p.m.

Farther along the Altmuehl toward the Nuernberg-Munich autobahn you'll come to Kipfenburg Castle but it's privately owned and visitors are not permitted.

Your next stop lies farther along the Old Mill Stream but it's best to go cross country and save 10 miles if you're intent on "conquering" the next burg just outside Riedenburg.

There you'll find a castle and a ruin, practically side by side.

On the right of the highway, up in a grove of trees, nestles the Burg Rosenburg. It's privately owned but groups of 12 to 15 are welcome to tour the schloss if they call in advance. Smaller numbers may look the grounds over and, perhaps, be shown the cellar cafe.

The next hill to Rosenburg's also has a castle, Rabenstein Schloss. But, unless you enjoy poking through ruins or letting the kids get a bit of exercise, forget it.

Riedenburg is now behind you and the road to Kelheim tries vainly to follow the winding river through the forest—

dark pines with a salt and pepper sprinkling of birches.

Far ahead on a jagged granite cliff guarding the north side of the valley a cream-colored castle perches on the rocks. This is Burg Prunn, a state-owned structure open from April to September from 10 a.m. to 6 p.m. and in winter from 10 a.m. to 4 p.m.

The castle heights, reached by a devious auto route from the village of Prunn, offer a splendid panorama and a spacious restaurant where you can snack or have a full-course dinner while enjoying the view.

Once a fighting burg with drawbridge and outer defenses (now gone), Prunn was converted into a residence when gunpowder finally changed the style of warfare.

Bare, wide-planked floors and sparse furnishings are Prunn's keynotes but it has been kept that way since Ludwig I of Bavaria put it under state protection more than 100 years ago. As a guide put it, "One cannot assume that in the old days they had much in the way of furniture — it was a barren, cold life."

But there's a Baroque chapel, rebuilt in 1692, faded murals in places where the layers of paint have been removed, a torture chamber (it may have only been a butchering room), a bit of armor, kitchen and ladies wing (1604 vintage), drinking and court rooms and curiosities like some late-Gothic chairs.

First written records of the castle put its beginning at 1037. The keep, square and still solid looking, was begun in the 12th century.

Prunn, like most of the other Altmuehltal castles, suffered during t h e Thirty Years War while under the control of an imperial field marshal. The damages were finally repaired when a band of Jesuits bought the castle in 1672.

Should you get hungry again at this point, journey on a few miles toward Kelheim to Burg Randeck, a ruin looming high over the highway on the left. You can drive up to the castle, park at the restaurant and enjoy some of the local delicacies while contemplating what's left of a Swedish "smorgasbord" of the 1630s.

Long before you near the juncture of the Old Mill Stream and the Danube, you'll see the top of a giant structure rising above the treetops ahead. It's the Befreiungshalle (Freedom Hall), one of Germany's most famous monuments.

Built under the direction of the same Ludwig I who had Burg Prunn restored and preserved, it stands nobly on the peninsula formed by the juncture of the Danube and Altmuehl.

You won't want to miss this architectural wonder which perfectly caps off a trip down the romantic Old Mill Stream.

Burg Prunn was converted into a residence when gunpowder changed warfare.

ELLINGEN:
Stronghold of the Teutonic Knights

GERMANY is said to have more than 20,000 castles within its borders — that's one castle for every 2,700 people in the federal republic.

Vast areas of Germany haven't even the semblance of a romantic ruin while other parts are absolutely infested with those relics of medieval days. But you can't tell them apart without a parchment scorecard.

One such area with more than its share, perhaps, of castles lies in Bavaria south of Nuernberg. There, you can scarcely drive 10 miles without coming within range of one.

Three of the closest to Nuernberg run in a direct line south on Highway 2.

They are the 16th century Schloss Ratibor in Roth; Ellingen where the once-mighty knights of the Teutonic Order held court; and the Wuelzburg Fortress, a "modern" castle built for the age of gunpowder on a hill southeast of Weissenburg.

Built in 1535, Ratibor has less than a romantic history. It never underwent siege as it was built in a difficult-to-defend position and was designed more as a jagdschloss (hunting lodge) and residence than anything else.

Count George of Ansbach built the schloss from profits reaped from an inheritance.

Schloss Ratibor is to be visited only on weekends. It's open Saturdays from 2 to 4 p.m. and Sundays from 10:15 a.m. to noon and from 2 to 4 p.m.

The castle passed into the hands of industrialist Johann Philipp Stieber in 1791. Some 60 years later, the most beautiful rooms were ruined when the city converted them for use as courtrooms; the original walls, ceilings and floors were torn out.

This so distressed Wilhelm Stieber, a descendant of the 1791 buyer and himself a wealthy industrialist, that he bought the castle in 1892 and began its restoration.

Importing the best talent available, Stieber returned much of the castle to its former glory. The most noteworthy of all the rooms is the castle's big festival hall (Prunksaal), a glorious imitation of Baroque decoration.

Fifteen miles south of Roth on Route 2, you'll come to Ellingen Palace at the far edge of the town.

Copper rainspouts five stories up jut out over the facade like braces of missiles ready to fire. Behind the elegant front are 120-odd rooms but only about

Schloss Ratibor surprises many visitors with the grandeur of this great banquet hall.

128

20 plus the chapel may be viewed by the public.

If you should wonder what a palace of such proportions is doing in little Ellingen, be advised that in its day this was a center of great power, temporal and spiritual. Here was headquarters for hundreds of knights of the German Teutonic Order, a religious group with its origins in the Third Crusade of 1190.

Strongly Catholic, this g r o u p of knights wielded great authority in an area which, at one time, reached all the way from the Main River to the alps and from the Rhine to the Inn River.

In 1552, Albrecht Alcibiades, count of Kulmbach-Brandenburg, charged through and burned and laid waste to the countryside and Ellingen Palace. It was rebuilt only to be plundered again by the Swedes in the Thirty Years War.

In 1815, King Max I of Bavaria gave Ellingen to Field Marshal Carl Philipp von Wrede and, in recognition of his service in the field (79 battles), made him the Prince von Wrede.

The prince restored much grandeur to the old palace, redecorating and buying back paintings and furniture which had been sold or taken away.

It is open winter and summer but with reduced hours during the cold months of the year when few people are willing to stalk the cold stone corridors.

Wuelzburg C a s t l e is just south of Weissenburg on Highway 13. Although you'll find no museum in it — the buildings are utilized for a school and an old folks home — it's worth a visit for several reasons.

It has the deepest castle well in all of Germany — 539 ft. And it is one of the few examples existing of a "modern" 16th century castle.

It took 16 years for Count Georg Friedrich's Ansbach men to build the fortress (1588-1604) and, when the Thirty Years War broke out, he sent his family there for safekeeping. But when Gen. Johannes Tilly's army appeared, t h e castle surrendered without a shot being fired — perhaps out of fear for the count's family.

At any rate, the Catholic army invested the fortress and, despite repeated sieges by Protestant forces, held on through the rest of the war.

The Wuelzburg is laid out like a five-cornered star with a 23-foot-deep, 75-foot-wide moat running jaggedly around the "star." At each "point," towering bastions loom over the moat, their flat tops carved out to accommodate cannon and riflemen.

Scrapping cupids appear in silhouette before the chapel of Ellingen Palace.

Knights of the Teutonic Order once took sacraments in elaborate chapel below.

REGENSBURG:
The Road to Valhalla

THE DANUBE may be blue only in the mind's-eye of romantics but this mighty stream wends through some beautiful country in Bavaria, bubbling along past castles and palaces on its way.

The stretch between Regensburg and Passau is hailed by Germans as among the most picturesque along its 1,750-mile course through eight countries to the Black Sea.

At Regensburg, the river flows beneath the arches of Germany's oldest bridge, a squat stone structure built in 1135.

How old the city is, nobody knows for sure. Long before the slave traders of the Middle Ages made fortunes for Regensburg merchants, Romans had their fortified Castra Regina there and hundreds of years before that peaceful Celts founded a village on the same spot which they named Rathaspona.

Palace of the Thurn and Taxis family was a monastery until 19th century.

Since 1748, Regensburg has been the residence of the princes of Thurn and Taxis who make their home in the St. Emmeram's Palace. The palace was a monastery until the secularization of 1808 and derives its name therefrom.

Noted for its museum and library, the palace's collection of antique carriages will probably be the high spot of a visit. Ornate wedding coaches, stagecoaches a la Wells Fargo and post coaches of the 19th century are among them.

It might be well to mention that the Taxis family at one time held the mail franchise for much of Bavaria, hence the post coaches on display.

A number of rooms in the Renaissance palace—throne room, banquet and dance halls, the mirror room and salons, for example—are open to the public. It is closed on Saturdays, however, and opens on Sundays from 10 a.m. to 11 a.m. Weekday tours are available.

Northeast of Regensburg there's a haunted castle you may want to take in before cantering away. Little Wolfsegg Castle, once the home of robber barons, has a "white lady" who is said to frighten the local people.

According to the story, the lady of Wolfsegg had a lover who was discovered by her husband. She is said to have stepped between the quarreling men just as her husband was stabbing her lover. The poor woman's soul found no rest (we are told) and her apparition roams the cold corridors and lonely ramparts.

For a little more substance to your legends, drop by the ruins of Donaustauf Castle overlooking the Danube a few miles south of Regensburg. Other than a good view—you can see all the way to Straubing in the south on a clear day—and a windy look at crumbling walls and arches, there's not much to look at.

Once numbered among the mightiest fortresses on the Danube, Donaustauf put up a determined defense when besieged by the Swedes in 1634. But the Swedes were just as tenacious as the Germans and the bitter battle ended in the destruction of the castle and the capitulation of its garrison.

From Donaustauf, where the towers were once so high that birds are said to have flown into them on foggy days, you can have a superb view of the

Donaustauf was blasted by the Swedes.

Great heroes of the German-speaking world are honored by busts at Valhalla.

Valhalla — Germany's great monument to its heroes of yesteryear.

Built by Bavaria's King Ludwig I between 1830 and 1842, the Valhalla was created in imitation of Greek and Roman temples. Fifty-two fluted marble columns surround the Parthenon-like building containing the busts of 116 German-speaking notables.

The interior is as magnificent as money and the talent of fine architects and sculptors could make it. Marvelous warm shades of marble and lavish gilding give the interior a harmony of tone wholly befitting an atmosphere of respect and homage.

Barbarossa, Frederick the Great, Luther, Beethoven, Schiller, Schubert, Goethe—they're all there.

Whether you're on a castle tour or whatever, you'll not want to miss this impressive sight.

Passau:
Sieges by the Score

WANT TO STAND on battlements where Napoleon once scowled in the direction of Austria? Or sleep in a burg which was blasted and conquered 15 different times?

If the answer is yes, then go to Passau where there are enough medieval delights to captivate the most discriminating of burg buffs.

This Bayerischer Wald (Bavarian Forest) area of southeastern Germany teems with little and big castles but most of them are in ruins or converted to private uses. Despair not. Passau itself offers two castles and a palace worth your while, and, if these are not enough, Neuburg Castle is only a skip down the road and you still haven't touched a number in the forest to the north.

Passau's Niederhaus Castle was built where the Inn and Ilz Rivers meet the Danube, a fact which has often resulted in catastrophe.

Marks left on houses show that, when the Inn and Danube reach flood stage at the same time, floodwaters 30-33 feet above normal have inundated the city.

The origin of the Niederhaus (Lower House) is wrapped in obscurity but was probably in the 13th century, although some chronicles mention the site much earlier. The present buildings date from after 1435; the keep, originally much higher, was chopped in half by Napoleon's troops in 1809.

The castle belongs to Mrs. Mathilde Brunner whose first husband, Eduard Strobelberger, bought it for her in 1907 shortly after they were married. She has lived there since that time.

The walls are nearly 10 feet thick. To offset the clammy chill in winter, Mrs. Brunner had central heat installed in the nine rooms she uses. There's also a modern bath and a valuable collection of antique furniture, paintings and artifacts.

Though it's not open to the general public, Mrs. Brunner enjoys showing guests her castle and its treasures. Americans are especially welcome: "They're more appreciative of the old things," she said.

Protected on three sides by water, the rear of this water fortress is guarded by the Oberhaus (Upper House) Castle, 300 feet above on the Georgs-

Niederhaus Castle is on point between Ilz and Danube; Oberhaus is at upper right.

Oberhaus Castle museum has an exhibit case of 16th century toys of wrought iron.

berg. The two are connected by a fortified wall built in 1343 by Bishop Gottfried von Weisseneck to strengthen the defensive complex around the Oberhaus.

Like the mighty churchmen of Salzburg who fled to the Hohensalzburg fortress in times of stress, the prince-bishops of Passau used the Oberhaus as their refuge. And it saved them on many an occasion.

From the year 1217, when Ulrich II was raised to the rank of prince-bishop, until 1803, Passau remained an independent principality. It was one of the largest bishoprics in the medieval Holy Roman Empire, with a sphere of influence stretching from near Garmisch to Hungary.

But Passau was also an important economic center and rose to prominence in part due to its advantageous position at the junction of three rivers. Passau swords stamped with the town's wolf's head crest became known throughout the world.

An uprising in 1298 forced Bishop Bernhard to flee. Up he went to the Oberhaus and his catapults unleashed a

Small mortar defended the Oberhaus.

rain of stone balls and burning tar on the city below.

The citizens were forced to capitulate but at least won a revision of the criminal and civil codes.

Several more times during the succeeding decades, Passau's townsfolk rose up against the bishops but always the mighty Oberhaus Castle beat them down, its engines of war (and later cannon) literally pointed down their throats.

It was not until the 15th century that citizens managed to get their Rathaus and some semblance of self-rule.

An Austrian army managed to storm and take the castle, defended by a weak garrison, in 1805. However, as Napoleon and his army appeared on the horizon, the Austrians withdrew. Napoleon thereupon made Passau his principal supply depot, put a Bavarian general in command of the Oberhaus and ringed the castle with five bastions and connecting walls.

The Austrians laid heavy siege to the castle in 1809 but eventually were beaten off.

Since 1932 the property of the city of Passau, the Oberhaus Castle draws many visitors to its youth hostel, camping site, picture gallery and museums. Sprawled across and over the sides of the Georgsberg, the citadel has a parking lot near its upper side.

A fine collection of two-handed swords, some 14th century cannon, battleaxes, suits of armor, Biedermeier furniture, medieval costumes—some of the ladies' styles have since come back in style—religious artifacts, a chemist's shop, bakery, blacksmith shop, spinning, weaving and carving equipment and a 14th century chapel with frescoes and an onion-top tower are among the things to be seen.

The picture gallery upstairs in the palace wing is an attraction in itself.

What else is there to see in Passau? Well, if palaces are your cup of mead, try the New Palace in town, one of the finest residences in Europe. It boasts an impressive staircase and a richly ornamented interior.

You also may want to look in on the Passau Cathedral, a superb Gothic church with onion-top towers and a Baroque interior of truly staggering beauty. The cathedral also has the largest pipe organ in Europe.

Dreiburgenland (The Land of Three Castles) has the Saldenburg, Englburg and Fuerstenstein Castles but none are open to the public. The Saldenburg houses a youth hostel; Englburg is a rest hotel with rooms to let; and Fuerstenstein is a Catholic Internat school.

In the other direction, some four or five miles south of Passau on the banks of the Inn River, stands Neuburg Castle. Among the oldest of Germany's castles, Neuburg was put up between 950 and 1158 by the various counts who ruled the region.

Spiked drop gate was part of the oft-conquered Neuburg Castle inner defenses.

Statue of a dwarf who lived in Neuburg during the 17th century.

It was not to be a happy place. Wars swept over the west banks of the Inn on 15 different occasions and each time the castle succumbed.

Admirably situated to repel attackers from the stream side—its battlements perch on steep cliffs nearly 400 feet above the river—it was less than well protected from attack from inland.

From the sad ramparts, there's an enthralling view of the Inn River Valley and also a view of the Austrian village of Wernstein on the opposite bank, with its ruined castle and Roman relics.

Today, the castle has been restored somewhat to its former condition. Much was lost in a fire in 1810 but the nucleus was restored in 1908 as a monument to the past. Present owner is the Munich Art Association, which maintains 45 rooms to rent to tourists. Furnished in Biedermeier and Baroque styles, some of the rooms are well worth seeing.

Several rooms are ornamented with lavish Italian terra cotta dating back to the early 16th century. They are said to be the only such rooms in Bavaria. Nicholas von Salm, one of the defeaters of the Turks at Vienna in 1529, gets credit for having ordered this fine work.

Also in the museum section of the castle are carloads of Roman relics, Celtic statues, oven tiles, sandstone gravestones, millwheels and a sculpture of a 17th century dwarf who is supposed to have lived in Neuburg.

The "engagement room" may take the fancy of the ladies visiting Neuburg. It was there that Emperor Leopold of Austria and Eleonore of Pfalz announced their engagement in 1675.

It's quiet in Neuburg—that is, in the castle and in the little town which bears the same name—and this might be just the spot to stop overnight while on a junket through to Austria. But not in winter—it's closed from November till April.

NYMPHENBURG:
Munich's Masterpiece of Many Mansions

Nymphenburg with its parks and fountains is a residence of splendid proportions.

Banquet Hall's glorious frescoed ceiling has nymphs, goddess Flora.

"IN MY FATHER'S house are many mansions."

Maybe the Bavarian monarchs weren't such regular readers of the Bible as to have come across this quotation in the Gospel of St. John but they certainly followed the example.

Ludwig II of Bavaria, known to many as the Mad King, was noted for his extravagant architectural creations of the 19th century but he had predecessors who set the pace a couple of hundred years before.

A good example is the Nymphenburg on the outskirts of Munich, the spacious summer residence of the rulers of Bavaria, built on the grand scale of Versailles.

As for the "many mansions" bit, Nymphenburg is anything but a single-unit palace on the order of those at Bayreuth or Ansbach, for example. It consists of a dozen or more separate parts—some joined into the main complex of buildings and some situated hundreds of yards away in surroundings designed specifically for them.

The history of Nymphenburg goes back more than 300 years to the time of Adelaide of Savoy, wife of Elector Ferdinand Maria of Bavaria. (Ferdinand was a king in his own right; in the Holy Roman Empire, those with the power to vote for the emperor of this loose federation of states were called electors.)

The nucleus of the palace is a five-story villa built for Adelaide by Agnosti Barelli of Italy, a leading architect of the day, beginning in 1664.

Adelaide played an important part in the planning of the square-shaped main building, specifying the features of

Gilded figures adorn coaches in what was the palace's former stables.

Ludwig II's extravagant coach is Marstall Museum's big attraction.

palaces and villas she had seen (especially Italian ones) which she wanted incorporated.

The simplicity of her summer residence did not please Adelaide's son, Max Emmanuel, who inherited the property on the death of his father. But, perhaps out of loyalty to his mother, he did not disturb what she had done, but rather added pavilions and arcades in symmetrical fashion on either side.

Wings were extended and soon the residence had taken on the shape of a rectangle.

The magnificent Baroque gardens laid out along a central axis running from the palace were also built during the reign of Max Emmanuel. The elector imported (courtesy of Louis XIV) a talented French landscape engineer who installed the canal system, pumps and basins with their many fountains, and trimmed hedges and formal gardens for which the park is now famous.

In the 19th century, the gardens were modified to conform to the style of English gardening then popular but the nucleus has remained much as it was.

Many refinements were added during the reigns of Elector Karl Albrecht (1726-45) and Elector Max III Joseph (1745-66), including interior stucco work by the famed J. B. Zimmermann and his son Franz.

But it was Max Emmanuel who had the elegant outside staircases added and gave the facade its classic appearance. The high arched windows put in the center let light into the big banquet hall which now rose through two stories.

It is in this magnificent hall that tours of the palace begin.

When the visitor looks up to the richly decorated ceiling, his eye is immediately caught by a fresco showing the goddess Flora receiving the homage of her nymphs—a reminder of how Nymphenburg got its name.

A dozen rooms are open to the public and they're done in a wide variety of styles, ranging from French Empire and Regency to Baroque and Chinese Lacquer.

The North Gallery has a series of paintings depicting the palace as it appeared during various stages of its development. They provide a valuable record of the original appearance of the place.

The South Pavilion houses the Schoenheiten Gallery—a collection of 19th century "beauty queens"—and a bedroom where "Mad King" Ludwig was born in 1845.

Emerging from the palace proper, one is struck immediately by the lovely expanse of lawn, flowers, topiary, trees and fountains—all bounded by a distant crescent of wall along which are spaced the many fine mansions built by Elector Karl Albrecht for important members of his court.

To the right from the same vantage point are the royal stables, now called the Marstall Museum.

Here, carefully preserved behind

Nymphenburg's Marstall Museum has one of the finest collections of sleds to be found anywhere in all of Europe.

Gilded nude hoids twin lanterns which permitted night use of sleds.

Ludwig II was fond of night rides on his sleds as shown in this painting.

glass, are saddles, bridles, reins, couplings, collars, traces and all the elaborate equestrian accoutrement a monarch needed to outfit his horses and carriages.

There's also a wide assortment of carriages: a tiny garden caleche; an English park carriage of 1800; gilded coronation coaches; the ponderous vehicle in which Elector Karl Albrecht rode to his crowning; Ludwig II's extravagant golden chariot; and plenty of other coaches and carriages used over a span of centuries.

The museum's fine collection of sleds is believed unequaled elsewhere in Europe.

These sleighs were pulled by horses in parades, weddings, state ceremonies and even coronations. They were also used for fun and games, especially by women and children, and, of course, as a means of transportation in winter.

So, you've finished the museum and the palace but that's not the end. No, indeed. You've still got four or five more things to see and they're all worth the time and effort it takes.

First, feast your eyes on the lovely area (the Parterre) behind the palace. The dozen or so white marble statues there were carved under orders of Elector Max III Joseph in the late 18th century. They're placed under protective cases during the winter (as are the dozens of others sprinkled about the park) so it's best to see the gardens in summer when the flower beds also enhance the beauty of the scene.

A large canal stretches into the distance toward the marble-lined cascades. Two large lakes adorn the park as well but they're not visible from the palace.

On the north side of the park, close to the palace, lies the Magdalenenklause. The artificial ruins of the exterior were deliberately treated to resemble the primitive abode of a simple hermit. It was to have been Max Emmanuel's hermitage and chapel but he died before it was finished.

Like the three other pavilions in the park, the Magdalenenklause was designed as a refuge from the strain of "modern" living and was modeled after the Trianons at Versailles.

From the chapel to the next pavilion is quite a hike through woods, across bridges and between flower beds. The Pagodenburg, as the name implies, is a small Chinese-type pavilion.

It faces the smaller of the two lakes flanking the cascades and was a tiny (diameter of 27 ft.) but charming place where Max could enjoy informal meetings and suppers. Food was prepared in a nearby kitchen and handed in through windows to be served in the Gartensaal.

For tea, the gentlemen and ladies usually went upstairs to the Chinese room with its parquet floor and Chinese rice paper tapestry. The unusual stairway between the two floors has walls lined with 2,446 Delft tiles, which harmonize beautifully with the color motif of the ground-floor rooms.

Across the two lakes from the eight-sided Pagodenburg, hidden by the trees in between, is the Badenburg—a luxurious bathhouse with apartments, banquet hall, play and dining rooms.

The pavilion fronts on the park's largest lake but it is doubtful that much swimming was done there since the Pagodenburg was equipped with a large swimming-pool sized bath. This lavish affair sports a crystal chandelier hanging directly over the center of the pool, marble slabs for wall paneling and a frescoed ceiling.

The fact that a balcony was built around the four walls over the pool indicates that this was a place for spectators and pleasure—not private bathing.

Bathing apartments were common in Max Emmanuel's day but a bathing house such as this is without parallel.

The last stop on your tour of the Nymphenburg park will be Karl Albrecht's hunting lodge, the Amalienburg, described as "the most perfect mani-

An exquisite Rococo interior makes the Amalienburg a first-rank tourist attraction.

Pagodenburg overlooks the quiet lake.

festation of Rococo art ever expressed in a garden pavilion."

It was the work of Francois de Cuvillies, a Walloon architect, decorator and engraver who was trained in Paris. He introduced into Germany the Rococo style then popular in France. The Residenz-Theater in Munich is the other most famous work of this dwarf who was one of the greatest decorative artists of the 18th century.

Hunting was most popular with the court in those days and it was at Amalienburg that the lords gathered before going out after pheasant and other game. The first room beyond the entranceway is, in effect, a kennel with individual stalls built into the paneled walls.

"Rover Rococo" might be the best way to describe it.

The following suite of rooms is a riot of lovely forms exquisitely decorated with rich silvered stucco work, paintings and mirrors. And the ladies will be overwhelmed by the kitchen—full stone floor and colorful wall tiling in bright Chinese designs.

Chinese room on second floor of the Pagodenburg was where lords and ladies had tea.

The Badenburg, a luxurious
bathhouse, is one of the garden's
four pleasure pavilions.

Boy on a dolphin
is a marble relic more than
200 years old.

SCHLEISSHEIM AND MUNICH:
A Gem and a Treasure

MOATS, drawbridges, fortifications and vantage locations are features of castles the world over. Munich's war-scarred Residenz is well worth visiting for the treasures and collections housed within its seemingly drab exterior.

Although it covers better than two square blocks almost in the down-town heart of the bustling Bavarian beer capital, it is not outwardly impressive—particularly if viewed from the bomb-battered side still surrounded by World War II rubble and weeds. But the Residenz is still as dear to Munich natives and Bavarians as Buckingham Palace and Windsor Castle are to Londoners and the English.

The palace has assumed the proportions of a small village in the very center of a modern thriving metropolis. The complex contains banquet halls, theaters, ballrooms, beautifully furnished state apartments, chapels and churches, and administration wings surrounding small but stately gardens and court-yards.

About six miles north of Munich, you'll find another monstrous-sized palace lay-out: Schleissheim's Neue Schloss (New Castle).

Schleissheim was Elector Max Emanuel's Baroque chateau, a lavishly appointed royal residence that developed from a hermitage built there by Duke Wilhelm of Bavaria. Max Emanuel had the first stones laid in the late 17th century.

Boasting extensive gardens and a long, clean facade, Schleissheim Palace has an interior to leave you gasping: a magnificent grand staircase; gleaming marble and delicate stucco work; a fine collection of frescoes and paintings; and beautifully carved doors.

The palace is open winter and summer every day of the week but the art gallery is closed on Mondays.

Munich's Residenz, however, is the place to go to see a real treasure chest of curios and rare antiquities. So, unless you want to save the very best for last, the Schatzkammer is likely to be the starting point of your visit. With more than 1,300 pieces, the Schatzkammer easily holds its own with the four other large treasury chambers which have survived the decline of European dynasties. The others are Dresden's Royal Palace and Albertinum, Vienna's Imperial Schatzkammer, the English Crown Jewels in the Tower of London, and the Kremlin collection.

Established by the Wittelsbach rulers, fondly remembered by Bavarians as discriminating collectors of lavish works of art and antiques, the collection, spread over 11 rooms, features a 1590 equestrian figure of the Knight of St. George, patron of the House of Wittelsbach. It is ornamented with 2,291 diamonds, 406 rubies and 209 pearls. Almost unnoticed beneath the horse and its bright blanket of jewels is the dragon, all the more monstrous for its emerald scales and ruby warts.

Despite its fame the Schatzkammer is only a small part of the Residenz Museum, first opened to the public in 1920. Although 75 per cent destroyed by Allied bombing raids during World War II, the Residenz is being rebuilt bit by bit and is expected to be completely restored in another 10 to 15 years. Most of the furniture, tapestries and other priceless collections were saved by storing them in caves, other castles and monasteries and in the Berchtesgaden salt mines for safekeeping during the war. Many items are still stored in scattered depots.

Extensive reconstruction was started in 1956. The Cuvillies Theater was the first part to be reopened, on June 14, 1958. This Baroque gem is now the scene of regular performances by the Bavarian State Opera.

That's the modern chapter in the history of the Munich Residenz. The beginning goes back to 1255 when Ludwig the Stern, upon partition of the Dukedom of Bavaria, transferred the government of his portion from Landshut, the seat of the Wittelsbachs up until then, to Munich. The first ducal residence was erected on the northeast corner of the oldest town wall.

Originally a fortified castle, it became a modest palace and town residence for the ruling Wittelsbachs, who were the first rulers in Germany to abandon their castle for a city residence constructed on stately and elegant lines. It was the cultural and intellectual focal point of the country in addition to being the heart of the administration.

East facade of the big Schleissheim Palace looks out on tree-lined formal gardens.

Duke Albrecht V started the museum business when he erected the Kunstkammer to house his growing art collection in 1563-1567. It is now the mint and is separate from the Residenz.

Two years later, the duke ordered construction of the Antiquarium, the first really important Renaissance building on German soil.

Today, this magnificent arched marble hall—despite a direct bomb hit which left it gutted in 1944—is often the scene of state receptions and banquets. But in 1571 it was destined to house Albrecht's library and collection of statuary.

Even before the original Kunstkammer and Antiquarium were completed, Albrecht had created a foundation establishing the Schatzkammer so that he would be remembered as a leading patron of the arts. It grew, particularly under the reign of his grandson Duke Maximilian I (1597-1651). Maximilian enlarged the collections, not so much as a patron of the arts, but as a status

The palace's glorious grand staircase.

The arched Antiquarium, built by Duke Albrecht V, is now used for state banquets.

symbol manifesting his new and exalted position as the first Bavarian elector, competing with monarchs from Madrid to Moscow.

Maximilian's grandson Max Emanuel contributed the spoils won from the Turks as defender of the West at Belgrade and Vienna.

Fresh interest was furnished by Emanuel's pompous son, Elector Karl Albrecht (1726-1745) who reveled in demonstrating the glory and wealth of the house of Wittelsbach. He added the Reiche Zimmer, a series of apartments considered today as one of the most important achievements in the entire sphere of German Rococo. The ground floor features the ornate ancestors' gallery, with 121 portraits of the Wittelsbach forebears. The apartments, opened on the elector's name day in 1737, were illuminated by 2,000 candles.

Various rulers made changes and added sections. The last change was in 1896 when Prince Regent Luitpold added a new treasury.

The Schatzkammer and Residenz collections were almost doubled when

Jewel-studded St. George slays dragon.

Ornate gallery contains 121 oil portraits of members of the House of Wittelsbach.

treasures of the Palatine-Zweibruecken branch of the Wittelsbachs were transferred from family palaces at Heidelberg, Duesseldorf and Mannheim.

The Residenz Museum is closed Mondays although the Schatzkammer is open every day.

Unusual 14th century English crown.

Munich Residenz' Cuvillies Theater.

HERRENCHIEMSEE:
Gilded Luxury in the Lake

The Herrenchiemsee Palace, modeled after Versailles, is on a 750-acre island.

KINGS ARE meant to live in castles. To loll in gilded splendor is part of their heritage.

Not all monarchs have subscribed to this, but Bavarian King Ludwig II did, and he carried it out with a purple vengeance.

During his life, the bachelor king directed the construction of three lavish castles. All three reflected his taste for artistic extravagance and his mania to live the life of a recluse.

Neuschwanstein was built on a bleak mountain top near Fuessen. Linderhof was set in lonely woods near Oberammergau. Herrenchiemsee was constructed in the middle of an island in Germany's largest inland lake.

The king's extravagance grew with age. It reached its epitome in Herrenchiemsee, the castle that is a replica of Versailles Palace. The last of his pre-

tentious creations (1878-86), it was never completed. Ludwig's drowning at age 41 in Lake Starnberg put an end to his ambitious building program, which included at least two more projects—a Byzantine castle and a Chinese palace.

His elaborate plans for Herrenchiemsee, a 750-acre island in mountain-rimmed Chiemsee, provide a clue to his sentimental ties with the age of romanticism.

Ludwig bought Herrenchiemsee for the Bavarian government in 1873.

His action may have been hastened by reports that lumber speculators were about to turn their axes to the lovely island of lush beeches, elms, ashes, maples, poplars, chestnuts and birches.

The king's long-term plans called for the conversion of the entire island into a garden and park, but his scheme was only partially executed before his death.

Ludwig's decision to construct Herren-

Ludwig II — the "Mad King" of Bavaria.

chiemsee in the style of Versailles came after a visit to the great French palace in 1874.

For it was Versailles that symbolized Louis XIV and the glory and absolute power of the French monarchy which he craved. Indeed, Ludwig admitted he had been born too late, that he belonged to the 18th century.

A total of 12 designs were submitted for his scrutiny before the cornerstone of Herrenchiemsee castle was laid in 1878.

Work progressed at a rapid pace, despite the difficulty of transporting materials and hundreds of workmen and artists by boat to the island.

Ludwig's death curtailed construction, but most of his plans were completed.

The interior of the palace includes 22 rooms, corridors and staircases decorated in the ornate tastes of the king. Among them:

HALL OF MIRRORS—This 100-yard-long hall was to be used for banquets, balls and high affairs of state.

Decorated in marble and gold, with a floor of inlaid rosewood, it includes 17 door-like windows which are reflected in as many mirrors in the opposite door panels. The huge vaulted ceiling is divided into several parts, which display in nine large and eight small paintings the story of Louis XIV. Thirty-three crystal chandeliers which now can be electrically raised and lowered, and 44 candelabra make possible the illumination of the hall by 1,848 wax candles.

SMALL HALL OF MIRRORS—This hall contains walls of marble and mirror panels. Statues in four corners represent Europe, Asia, Africa and America.

The staircase is a beautiful marble creation.

Mirrored "America" in Small Hall.

The Great Hall of Mirrors is 100 yards of marble, gilding and fine inlaid flooring.

An unforgettable sight: illumination of the Great Hall with its 1,848 wax candles.

KING'S BEDROOM—The bed, railing and decorations on the walls and ceiling are hand-carved of wood and covered with gold leaf.

WORKROOM—The writing desk in this room is composed of different kinds of inlaid rosewood. It is a copy of the desk of Louis XV in the Louvre in Paris.

PORCELAIN ROOM—Almost the entire decoration of this room is made of Dresden porcelain, including four tables with vases and candlesticks.

DINING ROOM—A 108-candle Dresden chandelier is the central attraction. There is a dumbwaiter, which allows the table to be lowered via a huge hand-operated elevator. Because of his penchant for privacy, Ludwig designed the table so that he could be served his food without the personal attendance of servants.

BATHROOM—A circular swimming pool, lined with marble, this room is one of the coziest in the castle.

His extravagance while he lived, Ludwig's castles remain a testament to his fantastic dreams. In the years that have elapsed since his death, the attitude toward the castle-crazy king has mellowed. Visitors now come from the four corners of the globe to gape at his expensive toys.

Herrenchiemsee alone attracts nearly a half million tourists a year, 25,000 of them from the American-operated Chiemsee Recreation Area. Tours are operated to the castle from the recreation area lake hotel through most of the year. It's just a 25-minute boat ride from the hotel to the Herrenchiemsee boat dock—then a 15-minute walk to the castle and the dreamy, romantic world of Ludwig.

When Ludwig wished to dine, his table was raised through the floor from kitchen.

LINDERHOF:
A Cascade of Romance

THE BATTERED carcass of history is cluttered with the wrecks of tormented souls who sought solace in isolation. Bavaria's King Ludwig II (1845-1886) is a case in point.

A romantic and a mystic in an age of restless pragmatism, the king soothed his clash with reality in lonely communion with nature and extravagant art. He was particularly fond of the sound of falling water, and at Linderhof—one of his three fairyland castles—he used to sit in his bedroom and gaze out at a

Shaft of water looks like a cupid's arrow when it's seen from this angle.

cascade of water tumbling down the mountainside to the Neptune Fountain.

The fountain and the waterfall—both designed by the king—are just part of the incredible setting at Linderhof, Ludwig's favorite home and the only castle that was completed before he drowned in Lake Starnberg in 1886.

The smallest of Ludwig's castles, Linderhof is the richest in ornamentation. Of white marble construction, it is set in the Graswang Valley, in a green terraced park six miles southwest of Oberammergau under towering peaks of the Austrian and Bavarian Alps.

Richest and largest room in the castle is the bedroom—a masterpiece of Rococo design. The enormous bed (Ludwig's 6-foot-7 frame required a large bed) is covered with a blue velvet spread. The bed is separated from the remainder of the room by a richly carved balustrade. Door frames are of Italian marble. The

Linderhof is the most popular of all the three Ludwig castles — and the only one completed before his death.

View from terrace of Linderhof, looking toward fountain which spouts every hour.

fireplaces are French marble and there is a huge crystal chandelier.

The frescoes of the bedroom ceiling show French King Louis XIV, Ludwig's most admired monarch, riding in his chariot. The dominant bright blues of the frescoes are as bright as the day they were painted.

From his bedroom, Ludwig could gaze high above the cascade of falling water to a 6,000-foot peak. The king first became acquainted with the scenic surroundings of Linderhof as a small boy when he visited the area with his father. The site of a modest hunting lodge, it was named after a Linder family that had farmed there in the Middle Ages. Ludwig was impressed with the natural grandeur of the isolated lodge. Later, when he first conceived his fantastic scheme for the construction of castles, Linderhof was his first choice for a site. Between 1869 and 1879 an army of workmen completed the castle and the magnificent gardens and terrace which occupy more than 75 acres of surrounding hillside.

The grounds include a geyser-like fountain which spouts every hour, a Moorish kiosk where Ludwig idled away the hours smoking a chibouk, and the grotto, a sunken cave complete with an

Neptune Fountain is below the cascades.

Grotte
Maurifcher Kiosk

Ludwig enjoyed Wagnerian operas in his small grotto with its own artificial lake.

artificial lake where Wagnerian operas were staged for the king and his private audiences.

Because of its scenic setting, Ludwig spent more time at Linderhof than at Herrenchiemsee or Neuschwanstein.

At Linderhof, he carried his role of the romantic to its epitome. Like Prince Charming, he drove to and from the castle in the depth of winter in a golden Rococo sleigh, with coachman and outrider dressed in 18th Century costumes

Since his death, all three of his castles have become tourist attractions. And the public appears to exhibit the same tastes as the king. In recent years Linderhof has attracted more visitors than either of the other castles.

Interlocked initials L,
gilded and topped by a crown,
decorate the doors.

A lonely, brooding man, King Ludwig spent hours in his Moorish kiosk at Linderhof, smoking a Turkish pipe and wishing that he had been born 100 years earlier.

The monarch loved the sound of falling water and he built fountains by the dozens.

NEUSCHWANSTEIN:
Mad Ludwig's Swan Song

Neuschwanstein, Ludwig's fairytale castle, with Hohenschwangau in the background.

Seen from near or far, Mad Ludwig's splendid masterpiece stirs the imagination.

THERE ARE CASTLES and there are castles. And then there is Neuschwanstein.

And when you have seen Neuschwanstein—then you can quit right then and there.

You can go home with the picture of the slender spires imprinted in your mind—with all your childhood faith in fairy tales restored. For Neuschwanstein is a castle that looks like a castle ought to look.

Indeed, it may be the one castle in the world that looks better to the eye than it does in a travel brochure. Straight out of legend and myth, it rises like a medieval fortress from a craggy peak in the Bavarian Alps, 80 miles south of Munich near the Austrian border.

When seen from the distance—with the turrets rupturing the mist and an array of peaks in the background—it is easy to let the imagination run wild.

Suddenly there are knights in shining armor riding down the mountain. They are led by a tall, handsome man on horseback. The tall man, of course, is Bavarian King Ludwig II (1845-1886) the legendary castle builder.

Ludwig's a n c e s t r a l home, Hohenschwangau, sits solidly on lower ground between the lake and Neuschwanstein. From its chambers, the Mad King could watch the workmen as his dream castle's spires reached into the heavens.

And what better place to build a castle than the mountains above Hohenschwangau? Even as a boy, Ludwig was impressed with the lonely, forbidding beauty of the terrain.

Less ornate in interior decoration than Linderhof or Herrenchiemsee, Neuschwanstein owes its grandeur to its setting and to the perfect blending of materials with its rugged surroundings.

Rising like an extension of the mountain it soars above the alpine foothills and the plains to the west. To the south—toward the Austrian frontier—water from the high mountains crashes down the Poellat Gorge, a view that the king surveyed from his bedroom.

Ludwig personally supervised construction of Neuschwanstein, which went on for more than 17 years and was still incomplete when he drowned.

The foundation of the castle rests on a 3,300-foot shoulder of rock under towering peaks and above the distant farmland surrounding the town of Fuessen. From the base the gray sandstone fortress rises in graceful slopes. One-hundred-and-ninety feet above the entrance, the king used to survey the surrounding countryside from the northwest turret. From this elevation the viewer can see deep into Austria and can gaze out upon five lakes.

The interior of the castle was decorated in medieval German style, designed to symbolize and glorify knighthood.

The castle abounds with reminders of the swan and the peacock—Ludwig's

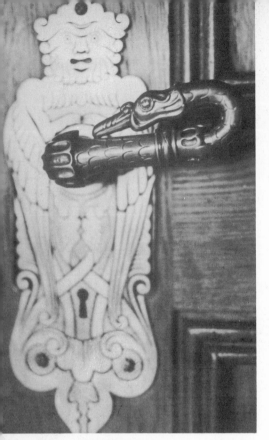

favorite birds. In one room the swan is depicted in huge, polished, wrought-iron door handles.

The most lavish private room in the castle is the king's bedroom—fitted with oak paneling which kept 14 carvers busy for four years.

The 45-foot-high throne room was never completed. This hall, decorated in Byzantine patterns, is the most ornate in the castle. Plans called for an ivory-and-gold throne which was never installed.

Model for the music hall, planned personally by the king, was the Singers Hall in the Wartburg in Thuringia. It is lit by 600 candles and has blue-and-red stained-glass windows.

A spacious kitchen—chiseled in the base of the castle—could have provided food for an army. Polished metal spits, an ice box and mammoth maple chopping blocks remain much the same as they were in the time of Ludwig.

Despite his preoccupation with the romantic, the king also liked modern conveniences and he equipped the castle with a number of new-fangled gadgets:

—A central hot-air heating system which piped heat into the throne room.

—A crude telephone system which connected Neuschwanstein castle with Hohenschwangau.

Swan motif is carried out throughout Neuschwanstein.

Porcelain swan (below) swims along by painted cousin.

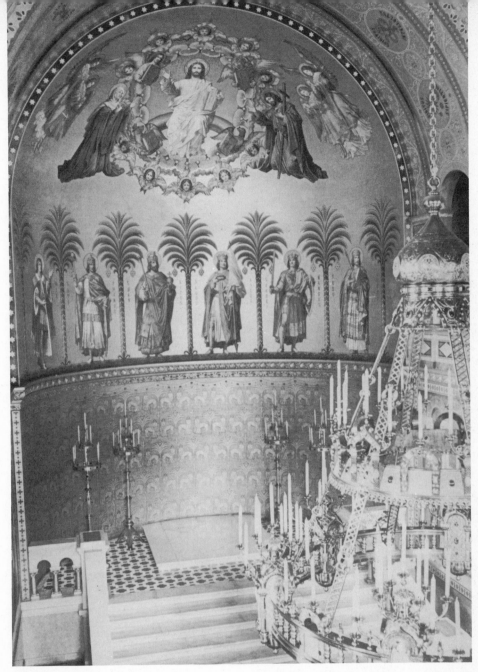

Mad Ludwig's gilded throne room in Neuschwanstein is still incomplete—no throne.

—An automatic toilet flush which used spring water from the mountains.

Since Ludwig's death, Neuschwanstein has been taken over by the Bavarian government. It is open all year.

Within catapult range of Neuschwanstein, Schloss Hohenschwangau was Mad King Ludwig's favorite residence and a castle restored by his father, Bavaria's King Max II, in 1833-1836.

In addition to its 700-year history, Hohenschwangau has a nice collection of period furniture, striking murals, armaments, a large assortment of oil paintings, wood carvings, icons, tapestries and curios from many centuries.

BERCHTESGADEN AND SALZBURG:
A Monastery, a Playful Bishop and a Citadel

JUST FOR KICKS, vary your storming of medieval castles with a visit to Hellbrunn Palace where the main storms are gales of laughter from delighted visitors.

You may get a little wet but it's all in fun and hardly anyone seems to mind the sprinkling jets of water which turn on and off unexpectedly.

If you're a blood-and-guts burg buff the trip needn't be a total loss, for within sight of the Hellbrunn fun fest is the Hohensalzburg Fortress, one of the mightiest medieval castles in Europe.

Both are within easy reach of the U.S. Recreation Centers at Chiemsee and Berchtesgaden. If you happen to be staying in Berchtesgaden, you may want to have a look at the 850-year-old castle there before taking in other sights.

Berchtesgaden Schloss, once an Augustin monastery, has been in the hands

The water-powered mechanical theater.

of the Wittelsbach family since the days of Ludwig I. The present head of the family, Albrecht, duke of Bavaria, lives in the castle at various times of the year.

It's open the year round, 9 a.m. to noon, Mondays through Saturdays, and conducted tours are available.

The castle offers ancient wood carvings, an armor collection and the largest set of antlers ever mounted in Germany.

From Berchtesgaden, the best route to the Hellbrunn Palace and Hohensalzburg is the "back road" toward Salzburg via Hallein. The trip takes 30 minutes and the border crossing is easier than at more popular points. Watch for signs pointing off to the left to Hellbrunn Schloss.

Hellbrunn Palace was built by Archbishop Markus Sittikus in only three years (1613-1615) as opposed to the Hohensalzburg which took hundreds of years to reach its current form.

Characteristic of the Italian late-Renaissance style, Hellbrunn is one of the few pleasure palaces to come down through the centuries in its original state, untouched by the vagaries of changing architectural styles.

But a word of advice: the palace opens at 8 a.m. from April 1 to Oct. 31 and the visitor who wants to see the water games, visit the palace building and gardens in a reasonable length of time should be there as early as possible. It closes at 6 p.m.

Night shows with floodlights on the leaping waters are held Tuesday and Friday nights in summer. In winter, the palace may be visited only by appointment.

Archbishop Sittikus, who was also the count of Hohenems, was a patron of the arts and, under his auspices, the earliest operas staged north of the alps were performed there. It is no accident that many of the statues in the gardens represent operatic characters.

First stop on the water games tour is the prince's banquet table — long, rectangular and marble — at which the good bishop could dampen spirits when parties got too lively or loud. A secret switch turned on jets of water guaranteed to drench everyone at the table — except the bishop.

Mischievous bishop could dampen spirits if his guests got out of hand at this table.

The mighty Hohensalzburg Fortress dominates the city from its towering perch.

Passing the lovely fish ponds and fountains on which the Orpheus Grotto faces, one enters the cellar of the palace building for a look at five interesting grottos. More than 100 springs come out of the Hellbrunn Mountain and the force of their water is used to power the devices found in the grottos and along the small canals.

The Ruin Grotto supposedly is where the archbishop took new guests by candlelight. One look at the "collapsing" ceiling and "sagging" walls and they fled in panic — right into the Neptune Grotto with its hidden jets of water or on outside where another series of sprinklers lay in wait.

The unwary (or unlucky) tourist may also get caught in these sprays; you never know when the water will be turned on or off or where it will come from next. The city-of-Salzburg-owned palace carries insurance to protect itself against law suits, however, brought by people who feel insulted or damaged by the water.

Children are charmed by the Birdsong Grotto where the chirping of 26 different kinds of birds is mechanically created by hidden water-powered devices.

Everyone is fascinated by the mechanical theater, however, and the guides voice drones on in a purposeful monotone as scores of tiny figures move about on stage. Organ music covers the low clanking made by the concealed

machinery and all is peaceful until, suddenly, water squirts everywhere!

The theater, built more than 200 years ago, depicts life in a typical town of the mid-18th century. It took four years to construct and is one of the palace's most prized treasures.

After seeing the water games, a pleasant walk around the fish ponds (teeming with carp and gold fish) brings you back to the palace. Rooms on the second floor are open to the public but the dining and concert rooms on the ground floor are not.

The big Festsaal (banquet room) has murals by Arsenio Mascagni, a Florentine friar who was the Salzburg court painter and who did many of the pictures in the Salzburg Cathedral. The long sides of this hall have brilliantly painted perspective views and when you cross it you gain the impression of having crossed a street.

Other rooms contain old pewter, cutlery, paintings of fish favored by the bishops, a Salzburg tiled oven (1608) with hunting scenes, tapestries, porcelain, glass and a portrait of the palace's founder, Archbishop Sittikus.

There's also a Chinese room with Oriental rugs and hand-painted wallpaper.

In a playroom, there's a representation of the famous "steer-washer" legend. According to the story, peasants were besieging the Salzburg castle in the 17th century and, since assault

Tourists cool their heels while the guide goes through his spiel at Hohensalzburg.

was impractical, they were trying to starve out the defenders.

The wily nobles, who were in fact running out of food, kept painting the same steer different colors and permitting it to be seen by the attackers. Thinking the castle garrison had a herd of cattle to live on, the attackers lost heart and drifted away.

A hundred yards or so from the palace and you're in the city of Salzburg. Drive on into town and look for a parking place in the old section of town near the foot of the mountain on which the fortress stands.

Around 900 A.D., the foundations for the first Hohensalzburg Castle were believed laid. However, this earlier date cannot be substantiated and the official beginning of this mighty lump of masonry is listed as 1077.

Possession of the castle was the key to the domination of Salzburg and the squabbling went on over the years, the losers generally ending up on the rack or one of the castle's many other gadgets designed to snap bones or separate the offending party from the truth or his limbs.

By 1365, gunpowder was in the headlines but this didn't worry the Hohensalzburg lords (yet). Cannon balls in those early days are said to have bounced off the walls like peanuts.

Written accounts by 16th century visitors to the castle describe in detail the extent of the fortifications and arma-

ments. Cardinal von Wellenburg wrote in 1514 of vast quantities of arrows, javelins, catapults, cannon and powder kegs.

Napoleon's men had no trouble taking the castle in the early years of the 19th century but their cannon shot harder than those which "bounced like peanuts" off the ramparts.

Now overrun by tourists, Hohensalzburg was once thought to be impregnable and, indeed, did withstand all attacks of armies using the old assault methods. It stands on the Moenchberg, 394 feet above Salzburg, and is reached by foot — not recommended for short-winded castle conquerors — or by the slow-moving funicular.

Once at the top, you'll be faced with a jumble of buildings to look through or at. A highlight, of course, is the museum with its rich endowment of armament, artifacts and instruments of torture and destruction.

Guided tours are available and make a visit more meaningful. You'll see old planked floors, a medieval courtroom, quaint courtyards, worm-eaten woodwork and an ancient pipe organ built in 1496.

If the Hellbrunn Zoo and palace and this sprawling fortress have exhausted you, finish up at the powder magazine and armory (now the restaurant) and enjoy a glass of local wine chilled in the cellars of the f o r m e r archbishops.

161

CELLE:
The Saga of Sophie

THE BEAUTIFUL Renaissance palace at Celle has enough international links to satisfy the United Nations. It was built by a German duke with a passion for architecture, was designed by Italians, and gave Britain its House of Hannover royal lineage.

The present palace was inspired by Georg Wilhelm, the last duke of Celle. The facade is heavy, Italian-influenced Baroque, the work of Guiseppe Arighini of Brescia, who was called in to complete the work started by a Venetian, Lorenzo Bedogni.

Georg not only liked Italian architects, but filled his palace with Italian works of art. Another Italian, Giovanni Battista Tornielli, built the heavily ornamented ceilings and fireplaces in the state rooms open to the public.

Georg and his wife Eleonore had one child—Sophie Dorothea—and it is to her unhappy life that Celle owes much of its historical significance.

Trying to find your way through the intertwined snarl of European royal interrelationships is something like translating Egyptian hieroglyphics into San-

Dating back to 1292, Celle Palace was originally built as a stronghold.

skrit, but it worked more or less this way:

Sophie was a bright, vivacious 16 when she married her cousin, Georg Ludwig, the heir-apparent to the House of Hannover. Georg Ludwig was a descendant of England's King James I and later ascended the English throne as George I. Apparently the cold, profligate Georg Ludwig made life miserable for the once-gay Sophie and the unhappy marriage ended 12 years later when he divorced her, after she had borne him two children, Sophie Dorothea and Georg.

Georg the younger later became George II of England and Sophie became the mother of King Frederick the Great of Prussia through her marriage to Wilhelm I of Prussia.

But back to the elder Sophie Dorothea. Her troubles were just beginning. After her miserable marriage ended, she planned secretly to leave the country with Count Philip Christoph of Koenigsmarck.

But Georg discovered the plan and the count disappeared. Sophie was exiled to Ahlden Castle, where she was kept until her death in 1726 at the age of 60.

Celle was first built as a stronghold by Otto the Stern, a duke of the powerful Brunswick-Lueneburg line, of the House of Guelph, in 1292. Of this structure, only the lower part of a huge tower, and the cellar vaults remain.

Of Georg Wilhelm's multi-roomed (Eleonore liked space) palace, only the chapel, theater and the state rooms are now open to the public.

Duke Georg had been a high liver too. Eleonore originally had been his mistress and the state rooms were once her private suite. But he finally acknowledged her as his legitimate wife in 1676.

The rooms have been redone in the florid, Rococo style of the period, though most of the artifacts are from other locations and eras. (A more complete selection of arms, armor, ancient uniforms and other historical memorabilia may be found in the Bomann Museum, across the street from the main entrance to the palace.)

Celle is a smallish town of about 60,000 population, located 20 miles northeast of Hannover in northern Germany. The palace is right in town and easy to find.

The palace theater was rebuilt in 1935,

but retains the shape, form and flavor of the 1600s. Georg Wilhelm liked Italian theater, too, and kept a band of Italian comedians around the house for entertainment.

The 319-seat theater, the oldest in Germany, still is used daily for performances.

From the artistic point of view, the chapel is the most interesting part of Celle Palace. The interior is exclusively Renaissance and includes a number of original murals which have remained untouched. The Gothic windows, however, are late 15th century.

The organ, its pipes encased in richly painted woodwork, dates from 1570 and is still used on special occasions.

Though the chapel originally housed Catholic services, it became a Protestant chapel with the accession of Ernst the Confessor, who brought the Reformation to the duchy.

Services are held there every Sunday from May through September. The chapel is not open during the cold months because the heating system that would be required would affect the delicate paintings.

The unhappy Sophie Dorothea, whose two children became world-famous.

Colorful Celle chapel is a remarkable monument from the Reformation period.

KASSEL: Gardens and Pinups

NOT BUILT for warlike purposes alone, the palaces and castles of the Kassel area, with their magnificent gardens and woods are monuments to the plush life of German nobility in the 18th and 19th centuries.

Best-known and most impressive is Wilhelmshoehe Palace on the outskirts of Kassel in Wilhelmshoehe Park, a hilly woodland converted over the years into a spot of beauty with fountains, rare trees and plants. It's all topped by the huge statue, grottoes and fountains of Hercules.

The palace's Weissenstein wing, built between 1786 and 1790 by Wilhelm IX, houses one of the largest collections of tapestries in the world. It consists of 20 rooms furnished with Hessian pictures, furniture and objects d'art from the 18th

The Hercules cascades and grottoes overlook plush Wilhelmshoehe Palace.

and 19th centuries. Particularly striking are the richly inlaid parquet floors.

For those inclined to oddities in interior decoration, there's a sunken, marble bathtub that must have been the last word in Saturday night ablutions. Only thing was, the tub had no drain plug and milady's ladies-in-waiting had to lug the water out as well as in.

Most of Wilhelmshoehe was built by Landgrave Wilhelm IX, who later became Elector Wilhelm I of Hesse. But the Hercules statue and its massive fountains were built in the early 1700s by Landgrave Karl.

Wilhelm was one of the most important rulers of the northern Hesse area, which was known as Hesse-Kassel. After the peace of Luneville in 1801, he was given some former French territory around Mainz and the title of elector. But he chose neutrality rather than joining the Confederation of the Rhine, an alliance proposed by Prussia. Napoleon threw out Wilhelm but the French, in turn, were thrown out after the Battle of Leipzig in 1813 and Wilhelm returned in triumph from exile in Bohemia.

Jerome Napoleon lived in the palace while Wilhelm was "out of town" and it was he who built the connecting colonnades and ballroom.

On Jan. 29, 1945, Allied bombs razed part of Wilhelmshoehe, but luckily the furniture and other memorabilia had been stored in safe places. The Weis-

Loewenburg knight still looks fierce despite damage to his arm and niche.

Wilhelmstal Palace, 9 miles north of Kassel, offers this gallery of "beauty queens."

senstein wing — less damaged — was rebuilt and reopened to the public in 1955.

Just around the corner — in the same park in fact — is the Loewenburg — Castle of the Lions.

Wilhelm built it in 1795 as a museum — a miniature Middle Ages Scottish castle, complete with drawbridge. It was built to resemble a ruin but, as the guide likes to point out, if Wilhelm had known the castle would be bombed in World War II, he wouldn't have had to go to all that trouble. Actually, the bombs destroyed only part of the tower.

Loewenburg houses a museum with an excellent collection of armor and weapons from the 14th to the 17th centuries.

The nobility of Hesse-Kassel must have been strong on lush parks and gardens because Schloss Wilhelmstal, 9 miles north of Kassel on Route 9, also is set in a beautiful park dotted with grottoes, fountains and cascades.

The building itself is considered a "pearl of the Rococo period." Though four prominent artists worked on its interior — Du Ry, Tischbein, Nahl and Ruhl — it is more harmonious than most other examples of the extravagant style. The gewgaw-and-curlicue Rococo style started in France, but the Italians and Germans of the period outdid its originators.

One of the best exhibits in Wilhelmstal is what may be the earliest playmate-of-the-year collection. Wilhelm commissioned Johann Tischbein and other artists to "each year bring back a painting of the most beautiful girl you can find." The results are hanging on walls of the palace's first floor.

Another Kassel area castle, for a leisurely drive through the rolling hills of the Werra Valley, is Berlepsch Castle. Take the Werratal turnoff, 10 miles north of Kassel on the Kassel-Hannover Autobahn, turn right to Gertenbach and follow the signs to Berlepsch. It is now an apartment house and restaurant.

Quaint exterior of Berlepsch Castle draws many for a look at the interior.

GOSLAR:
An Echo of Emperors

THE REMARKABLY well-preserved Kaiserpfalz at Goslar is a good bet for those who like their history out where it can be seen.

Murals in the massive Knight's Hall depict significant scenes from German history from Charlemagne's overthrowing the Saxons in 782 to the succession of Kaiser Wilhelm II in 1888.

The Kaiserpfalz — imperial palace — dates from the 10th century. It was built on the northern edge of the Harz Mountains at Goslar, probably because of the rich deposits of copper and silver ore nearby. From the 10th to the 13th century, it was the favorite court of Salic and Hohenstaufen emperors.

Situated 14 miles east of the Seesen turnoff on the Kassel-Hanover autobahn, the present structure is primarily a reconstruction of the great hall built by Kaiser Henry III, about 1050. The foundation remains intact.

It is considered the biggest and oldest imperial court in Germany—its main hall alone measures 147 by 49 feet. The medieval walls of this hall probably were originally hung with colorful tapestries but, between 1879 and 1897, Her-

mann Wislicenus created the murals which give the visitor German history at a glance.

The chapel housing the sarcophagus of Henry III was built by Henry V in the 12th century. The outer walls at ground level form a Greek cross but are transformed into a Byzantine octagon in the upper story.

The Kaiserpfalz murals may offer a picture history of Germany, but the palace has made its share of history, too.

Like the time in the 11th century when Abbot Widerad of Fulda tried a little power play to get a seat closer to the king at the imperial court. (Men of the cloth, in the old days, weren't too particular about steering clear of politics or secular ambitions.)

The good abbot had been feuding for months with Bishop Hezilo of Hildesheim about the court seating, and the bishop, with the help of Count Egbert of Brunswick, was determined to cut the abbot down to size. He wanted to demonstrate dramatically that no little abbot from Fulda was going to get pushy in his diocese.

The feud came to a head and trig-

The Kaiserpfalz at Goslar is considered Germany's biggest, oldest imperial court.

gered what came to be known as the Whitsuntide Trouble at Goslar.

The 13-year-old King Henry IV had come to Goslar in 1063 for the Whitsuntide holidays and on the day before the Sunday chapel service, a number of Egbert's knights hid behind the altar and routed Abbot Widerad's servants when they came in to arrange the chairs.

The combatants were quieted and the service began, only to be interrupted by Widerad's troops who burst into the chapel, swinging swords. Cries of the wounded filled the chapel and Bishop Hezilo mounted the pulpit, but only to act as a cheerleader for his followers.

"Sanctity of the church? Don't worry about that," he is said to have shouted. "I'll accept the responsibility."

The battle raged until nightfall, when the abbot's forces finally succumbed.

A royal court blamed Abbot Widerad for the trouble and he was fined heavily. Which meant that the plotter, Bishop Hezilo, and other church princes fattened their purses by sacking the rich abbey at Fulda.

Emperor Barbarossa on his trusty steed.

Henry III built the original Empire Hall, now boasting of fine murals, about 1050.

BERLIN:
A Castle Buff's Dozen

ALTHOUGH THE pace of West Berlin is very much dictated by the harsh facts of the present, memories of a regal past still have their place in the city's 12 castles.

If the number seems a little on the high side, the Administration of Castles and Gardens has them all faithfully listed, indexed and catalogued.

Admittedly, some would pass for mere manors elsewhere.

Take a place called Villa Borsig on Lake Tegel which once belonged to a Berlin steel tycoon and now houses a federal government agency.

Or Palais Pannwitz, the sumptuous habitat of Emperor Wilhelm II's lawyer, which has been converted into a plush hotel at the edge of the Grunewald woods.

But whether ritzy or plain, once a West Berlin building has been classified as a castle, it is accorded the protection given to all historical municipal monuments. No one dares relocate a geranium pot on the premises without getting an official okay.

This civic zeal can be explained, of course, by the ravages of the war which destroyed many historical buildings and by the fact that West Berliners no longer can go to East Berlin, which lists seven castles of its own.

Unfortunately, the only Schloss really worth its name and one which is always associated with Berlin — Sans Souci, the residence of Prussian kings — is located at Potsdam, just outside the city limits in East Germany proper.

Here are the 12 West Berlin castles listed in the official roster:

Charlottenburg Palace, Bellevue Palace, Grunewald Hunting Lodge, Peafowl Island Castle, Tegel Palace, Spandau C i t a d e l, Klein-Glienicke Castle, Glienicke Hunting Lodge, Rudow Hunting Lodge, Brueningslinden Palace, Villa Borsig and Palais Pannwitz.

The largest is Schloss Charlottenburg, named after Sophie Charlotte, the beautiful and high-spirited spouse of t h e Elector Frederick III, who was to become King Frederick I in 1701.

When construction began in the 1690s, plans called for a summer residence for Sophie, but with one expansion after another, it ended up a cavernous palace which occupied the talents of Prussia's leading architects.

Today, it contains West Berlin's National Gallery (19th and 20th century art), the Museum for Archaeology, and the Museum for Applied Arts.

The castle's main section — topped off by a copper-sheathed cupola — encloses historic rooms with valuable furnishings, paintings, tapestries and porcelain, most of which belonged to Frederick the Great, "Der Alte Fritz."

The king's spacious suite can be seen in the so-called Knobelsdorff wing, named after the architect who designed it.

The pivot point of the Charlottenburg courtyard is an imposing statue of the Great Elector, Friedrich Wilhelm, one of the best known examples of German Baroque sculpture.

The electors were European rulers entitled to take part in choosing the emperors of the Holy Roman Empire.

His equestrian statue, a work of Andreas Schlueter, once was a landmark gracing a Spree River bridge near the old Imperial Palace. During World War II bombing raids, it was removed from its pedestal to be moved to a safer lo-

Bellevue is residence of the West German president—when he's in town.

Charlottenburg Palace dates back to the 1690s. Named for Sophie Charlotte, it is Berlin's largest castle and contains an art gallery, two museums and many rooms.

cation. But the barge which carried it sprung a leak and sank. In 1950, the hulking monument was recovered and installed in its new place at Charlottenburg.

Another Schloss erected during the Prussian era was Bellevue in the Tiergarten park which, since 1959, has been the official residence of the president of the Federal Republic whenever he is in Berlin.

Bellevue was finished in 1786 as the residence of Prince August Ferdinand. It was heavily damaged during World War II. But, even though the building was painstakingly restored, it now contains little of historic interest. The public is admitted on Sunday afternoons when the president is not in Berlin.

More rewarding to castle hoppers is a tour of Jagdschloss Grunewald, a glorified hunting lodge on the wooded shores of Lake Grunewald. It is considered Berlin's last Renaissance structure and was

Porcelain and wood treasures (below) may be viewed in Grunewald Hunting Lodge.

Peafowl Island Castle was built a romantic ruin by King Frederick Wilhelm III.

built in 1542 by the Elector Joachim II, who used to hunt for boar in the area.

Although there is some antique furniture, the castle has become more of an art gallery, with works by Lucas Cranach the Elder and Younger, Rubens, Chodowicki and some Dutch masters.

Probably the most intriguing of West Berlin's small castles — historically and architecturally — is Schloss Pfaueninsel (Peafowl Island) which squats on the Havel River island of the same name.

The tiny island sheltered a rabbit farm in the 17th century before it was taken over in 1685 by an alchemist, Johann Kunckel von Loewenstern, who produced valuable ruby glass there for the Great Elector.

Four years later, the place was wrecked by an explosion, and for the next 100 years or so, the island's fertile soil provided the vegetable supply of a Potsdam orphanage.

During that time, it was occasionally used as a hideaway and picnic grounds by the Prussian royal family. In 1793, King Frederick Wilhelm II decided to have a small pleasure palace built there for himself and his mistress.

Going along with the romantic mood of the era, the castle was made to resemble a ruin, and a Gothic chapel facade hid a cow stable.

Peafowl Isle became known as a kind of regal Disneyland under the king's son, Frederick Wilhelm III, who populated it with exotic beasts which were free to roam the island.

He added a palm house, a rose garden, a playground, a dry-docked frigate (a gift of the king of England) and even a pair of giants and dwarfs, and opened the gaudy place to the gaping public. (In 1842, the animals were taken off the island to provide the basic stock for the present Berlin zoo.)

Peafowl Island was declared a state park in 1924 and has remained a favorite excursion goal for Berliners.

The castle, which has kept its 18th century interiors, is open from 10 a.m. to 6 p.m. from April 1 through September, and from 10 a.m. to 5 p.m. in March and October. A ferry shuttles visitors over from the Nikolskoe boat landing.

Tegel Palace and the Spandau Citadel are on the fringes of West Berlin.

Tegel, in the wooded suburb of the same name, has found its place in German culture as the former residence of Alexander von Humboldt, a famous scientist and explorer, and his brother Wilhelm, a Prussian diplomat.

The Humboldt castle, at the height of its splendor, was a meeting place of royalty and intellectuals, including Goethe and Schiller.

Originally a country mansion, the castle in 1821 was done over in the classic style of Karl Friedrich Schinkel, Germany's most famous 19th century architect. The castle has been converted into

Tegel Palace has antiquities like marble statues, frieze works among its treasures.

a museum, owned and operated by the heirs of the Humboldt family.

Spandau Citadel, near the junction of the Spree and Havel rivers, is the only medieval fortress in Berlin.

Spandau is older than Berlin and was first mentioned in 1160 during the reign of Albrecht the Bear, who allegedly gave Berlin his nickname. The bear is part of Berlin's flag and coat of arms.

Aside from its military purposes, the Spandau "Zitadelle" served at various times as a state prison, Prussia's Fort Knox, a weapons and munitions plant, and — during the Nazi era — as a poison gas laboratory.

The squat Julius Tower held the imperial war treasure from 1871 until 1914 when the 120 million marks in gold stored there financed the start of World War I.

The thick-walled tower and a small museum. where exhibits trace the history of Spandau and the fortress, are the most interesting parts of the citadel complex.

The fortress should not be confused with the Spandau prison nearby for Nazi war criminals sentenced by the Nuernberg tribunal.

It's quite a hike to the top of spiraling staircase in the Julius Tower in Spandau Citadel.

JOHANNISBERG AND VOLLRADS:
A Sip of History

ONCE THERE WAS a castle connoisseur who grew weary of sandstone battlements, medieval legends, halls full of armor and blunderbusses, cannon with the range of a BB gun, battleaxes and crossbows.

His glazed eyes were seeing Rococo where the stucco work and frieze ornamentation were obviously Baroque. He had seen so many museums, read so many books, talked to so many guides and written so many words on the subject of castles that things were running together in a blur of unintelligible facts.

Clearly, this was a buff who had had enough.

The boss, seeing the hesitant hand and the uncertain air, decided on a change of pace. Some sort of therapy was in order. The assignment: Johannisberg and Vollrads—two castles only a short distance upstream from Ruedesheim on the Rhine River.

No grape shot at these two castles — but plenty of juicy grapes, wine.

The jaded castle fancier found these two offered something none of the others had. To his delight, he walked into a world dominated by the noble grape.

Gone were visions of Middle Ages combat and Romanesque splendor. Found was a new zest for exploring the unusual and a chance to see Germany's famous Rhine wine in the making.

At the little village of Winkel, on the same side of the Rhine as Wiesbaden, you can turn off Highway 42 into the hills and find both of these castles. You take separate roads to reach them but they're almost within shouting distance of each other.

The vintner will be glad to let you watch the picking (Weinlese, they call it in German) and the pressing if you don't get in the way.

Pressing grapes is no longer done in the old way. At both Vollrads and Johannisberg Castles, you can see modern devices which squeeze out the juice using air pressure.

There are many similarities between Johannisberg and Vollrads. They are both called castles but you wouldn't think so to look at them.

Johannisberg looks more like a mansion some millionaire built atop a ridge to get a good view of the river and valley. Vollrads has a view too (though less impressive) but it's constructed more on the traditional plan of a medieval farm with enclosed courtyard.

Both are occupied by nobility and are not open to public inspection. The bishops of Mainz started the castles and the vineyards but they came into private hands eventually and have remained so.

Most of the wine that comes from their vineyards is shipped to the United States.

"Unfortunately, there's little left for local consumption," an official at Johannisberg said. He estimated that 60 to 70 per cent of that wine goes to the United States, most of it to the New York area. At Vollrads, the U.S. export percentage was estimated at a bit more than 30 per cent.

Schloss Vollrads' history covers more than 600 years. It still has the lovely gardens and square tower, which Goethe called "wunderlich."

Wine kegs, some in use for 100 years,

The vast cellars of Schloss Johannisberg contain hundreds of kegs of aging wine.

fill the cellars. Made of oak, many hold as much as 300 gallons. Wine mustn't be allowed to freeze, so there are heating pipes in case the temperature drops too low.

There are 10 cellars and all are damp. "The wine will evaporate through the porous kegs if stored in a dry place," a foreman explained.

Bottled wine is stored in a separate cellar in tight blocks of about 8,000 bottles each.

Johannisberg has a terrace (open from April to November) where the weary sightseer can rest while enjoying the fine view and the product of the vineyards below.

The castle has three vast wine cellars. Two date only from 1721 but the old cellar, deepest of the three, was dug in 1100.

Wine of high quality can be kept almost indefinitely and in the Johannisberg cellar samples of the wine for each good year since 1842 are kept under lock and key.

There are even two dusty, crusty bottles of 1748 Johannisberg.

Schloss Johannisberg got its start in the year 850 when Rhabanus Maurus, archbishop of Mainz, built a chapel on the hill in honor of St. Nicholas. In 1100, Benedictine monks built a monastery in its place, dedicating it to St. John the Baptist, and it's from the saint that the place gets its name of Johannisberg (John's Mountain).

The Benedictines greatly improved the quality of the Riesling vines and kept records of annual harvests. The monks discovered that allowing grapes to molder and harvesting them late made for a better product.

So, here's just the place to drink a toast to the castles of Germany.

So, here's a toast to the castles of Germany and home of the noble grape.

GLOSSARY

Abt—abbot
Abtei—abbey, monastery
Armbrust—crossbow
Bann—outlawry, ban
Bannbulle—bull of excommunication
Barock—Baroque
Bastei—bastion
Bau—building, wing
Bauernkrieg—Peasants War of 1524-1526
Berg—mountain; favored spot for locating castles was on a hill or mountaintop.
Biedermeier—a style of architecture and decoration popular about 1815-1840.
Bischof—a bishop
Bollwerk—ramparts
Brunnen—fountain, well, or spring
Burg—a defensive structure, castle or fortress, arranged around a keep (a tower or other strong structure designed as a place of last refuge).
Burggraf—count with the responsibility for a castle and its environs.
Burgschenke—tavern of the castle
Burgverliess—castle dungeon
Burgwarte—keep; watch tower
Chronik—chronicles
Denkmal—statue or monument
Deutschordensritter—Teutonic Knights
Drachen—dragon
Erzbischof—archbishop
Fachwerkhaus—timber-frame house
Fahne—flag
Fehdehandschuh—gauntlet
Festsaal—banquet hall
Festung—a fortress designed for defensive purposes; most often on a larger scale than a simple castle.
frei—free
Freiherr—baron
Freistadt—free town; one with its own charter and government.
Fremdenverkehrsamt (or Fremdenverkehrsverein)—official tourist office; an excellent source of information, usually in railroad station or city hall
Fuerst—prince
Fuerstbischof—a prince-bishop
Gemaeldegallerie—picture gallery
Geschuetze—big guns
gotisch—Gothic
Grab—grave, tomb
Graf—count
Grotte—grotto
Harnisch—armor
Hellebarde—halberd, a piked weapon
Helm—helmet
Herzog—duke
Herzogin—duchess
Hexenturm—witches tower
Hof—court or courtyard
Hofkapelle—court chapel
Irrgarten—maze
Jagd—hunt or hunting
Jagdschloss—hunting lodge or castle
Kaiser—emperor, as the emperor of the Holy Roman Empire
Kampfkeule—mace
Kanone—cannon
Kapelle—chapel
Keller—cellar
Kemenatenbau—ladies wing of a castle
Keuschheitsguertel—chastity belt
Koenig—king
Koenigin—queen
Kueche—kitchen
Kutsche—coach
Kreuzgang—cloister
Kreuzgewoelbe—cross-vault
Kreuzzug—crusade
Krieg—war
Kunst—art
Kurfuerst—an elector, as in the Holy Roman Empire

ARCHITECTURAL STYLES

ROMANESQUE — Characterized by a solid, rounded appearance, thick walls with few windows; barrel vaults, rounded arches and domes; 8th Century to about 1250.

GOTHIC — Light, airy, soaring, emphasizing vertical; pointed arches, ribbed vaulting; flying buttresses were developed to support walls and take part of the load; this permitted tall, narrow windows (often with stained glass), elaborate stone tracery and carving; highly decorated with statuary, gargoyles to hide rain spouts; approximately 1250 to 1500.

RENAISSANCE — A return to the horizontal on the grand scale; geometric layouts and designs; classical motifs such as columns, rounded arches and domes; free use of detail and patterns; 16th Century.

BAROQUE — Freer, with emphasis on curving lines; less rigid layouts; much emphasis on decoration; rich use of gilding, color, stucco work, frescos, marble, inlaid woods and paintings; 17th and 18th Centuries.

ROCOCO — Light, frivolous, with lots of playful detail; twisted curves; frequent use of shellwork and s h e l l patterns; artificial grottoes; 18th Century.

174

INDEX

(Turn page)

GLOSSARY

Land—state

Landsknecht—mercenary or hireling, soldier in the Middle Ages

Lanze—lance

Lustschloss—pleasure palace

Markgraf—margrave; an important count, one who usually had power over a large estate or territory, originally governor of a German border province

Marstall—horse stables

Mauer—wall

Minnesaenger—minstrel

Mittelalter—Middle Ages

Morgenstern—club weapon, sometimes made with a swinging mace head.

Muenzen—coins

Orgel—organ

Palais—palace (French)

Pechnase—projection on a castle wall from which defenders were able to pour boiling liquids on attackers.

Prinz—prince

Prinzessin—princess

Pulver—powder, as in gun powder

Rathaus—city hall

Raubritter—robber baron

Reich—empire

Residenz—an official residence, usually a palace

Ritter—a knight

Rittersaal—knight's hall; a castle room where the knights gathered to sleep and eat

Rokoko—Rococo

romanisch—Romanesque

Ruestung—armor

Ruine—ruin

Sammlung—collection

Schlacht—battle

Schlitten—sled

Schloss—a residence for nobility; usually a palace-type structure but also often used for a fortress or castle

Schmiedeeisen—wrought iron

Schwert—sword

Soeller—garret, balcony

Speer—spear

Springbrunnen—fountain or water-spout

Staat—state

staatlich—adjective of state, as in state-owned

Stadt—city

Stil—style, as in Baroque style

Tal (or Thal)—valley

Stuck—Stucco

Tor—gate; castle gates were fortified and often included a drawbridge

Treppenhaus—grand staircase

Turm—tower

Turnier—jousting tourney

Veste—another word for fortress

Waffen—arms

Waffenschmied—armorer

Wandgemaelde—mural painting, fresco

Wandteppich—hangings, tapestry

Wasserburg—moated castle

Wassergraben—moat

Wehrgang—a runway or gallery (located usually hanging on a wall just behind the parapets of a castle)

Zinn—pewter

Zinnen—battlements

Zugbruecke—drawbridge

INDEX
(Continued)

176